YOU
TALK TO GOD
LIKE THAT

YOU CAN TALK TO GOD LIKE THAT

THE SURPRISING POWER OF LAMENT TO SAVE YOUR FAITH

ABBY NORMAN

BROADLEAF BOOKS
MINNEAPOLIS

YOU CAN TALK TO GOD LIKE THAT
The Surprising Power of Lament to Save Your Faith

Cover design: Cindy Laun

Print ISBN: 978-1-5064-6906-5
eBook ISBN: 978-1-5064-6907-2

To my mother, whose faith taught me about
a God I could trust with my whole self

CONTENTS

PART ONE
LAMENT TO GOD

PART TWO
LAMENT IN COMMUNITY

PART THREE
PUBLIC LAMENT AS AN AGENT OF CHANGE

ACKNOWLEDGMENTS

I t takes a village to raise a child, and also to write a book (especially if you are also raising children). This is especially true if you are writing a book in the midst of a pandemic. If nothing else, the process of this book has reminded me of how rich I am in love and support. If you sent me treats or coffee, offered to watch my kids, prayed for me, or responded to my text messages and desperate tweets with sincere encouragement or ridiculous GIFs, know that I am so deeply grateful for you. This would not have happened without you.

To my internet safe places: Tanya, Beth, Jen, and all of Inkwell, thank you for believing in me even when I couldn't and for cheering me on every step of the way. Holly, Heather, Nicole, and all the Rise community, you got me a hotel room, you fed my kids and my parents, you sent me art. Abby, you prayed me right to the end of the finish line. You were the hands and feet of Jesus every time I needed to be held up the most.

To my Megans, Volpert and Westra: thank you for being the sage voice that consistently talked me down (Volpert) and the ridiculous gift giver just when I needed ten pounds of gummy bears or a mug with the F-word on it (Westra). Both of you just get me.

To Lizzie, Michelle, Danielle, and Alison: What would I do without people who answer every single one of my text messages with grace and snark in equal measure?

To my girls: I pray that the months of being told "Mommy is writing" will not scar you but instead inspire you. I would apologize for all the pizza, but you liked it.

Finally, to my husband, who supports me in all my endeavors: thank you. I was not a writer when I married you, but I am deeply grateful for your editing prowess. Let's keep making room for each other.

INTRODUCTION

"Honey, are you mad at God?" In that small sentence in our living room, her in the chair, me on the couch, my mom asked me about the one thing I hoped no one would ever notice. I was maybe seventeen and had been sick on and off for four years with what would eventually be diagnosed as fibromyalgia. I was also deeply earnest about my faith, the kind of innocent earnestness teenagers fall so easily into. I was a leader in my youth group and wore Christian T-shirts to school in the hopes of witnessing to my friends. I organized the prayer for See You at the Pole day. I was a good Christian girl. I didn't want anyone to know I was mad at God, but I was. I was really mad at God. I wanted to be good, and faithful, and sure of God. But I had been sick for so long, and it was only getting worse, and no one could figure out what was wrong with me. And 1998 was not a great time to be struggling with an autoimmune disorder. These days, everyone knows someone with fibromyalgia, chronic fatigue, or some other immunodeficiency, but when I was young, most people figured I was making it all up.

With even God ignoring my cries for healing, it felt like God didn't see my pain either.

Over the same four years that I struggled with my health, our church had a bit of a revival. The Holy Spirit showed up in miraculous ways. About once a month, I went to a prayer service and watched people be healed. On Sundays, we heard tales of a faithful God healing babies' asthma and shrinking tumors. Every single month, I walked to the front of the church and allowed people to lay hands on me with the sincere belief that this time, God would heal me. Every month, I believed I was healed and lived into that healing by insisting I was OK before collapsing into a pile of exhaustion when it became clear I was not. At the end of one of those heart-wrenching cycles, I dragged myself from my bedroom to the living room and fell into an aching heap on the couch. It was then that my mother asked me if I was mad at God.

When I think about that teenager now, in her gray marching band hoodie, crying in her living room, I am so grateful for what happened next: my mother saw me. I looked up at my mom, horrified that she knew my secret. I was very, very mad at God. I could not understand why God was letting me remain sick when I knew God had the power to heal. I had, for my whole life, been faithful to God, and now God was not returning the favor. How could God have forgotten about me? Why would God not heal me? Didn't God know I was in pain? Couldn't God see that I was suffering? I was so confused and angry with God, and I was terrified that being angry at God meant that I was bad. Good Christian girls praised God. They loved Jesus and talked about their faith and trust in him. I was sure being angry at God was the opposite of that—something that failed Christians did. I was sure being angry with God was not a choice.

My mom scooped me into her lap (well, sort of—I was at this point bigger than she was). She held me and rocked me and said what I think are the two most important sentences I have ever heard: "Me too. I am mad at God too." I completely dissolved into a puddle of tears. I was not going to be judged for my anger and sorrow. I was not alone in resenting an all-powerful God who refused to heal me. I was not the only one who felt like God had somehow forgotten me. I was allowed to be mad at God. I am so glad my mom was willing to teach me that. That lesson has saved my faith over and over again.

I was reminded of that moment almost twenty years later in my first year of seminary, studying the Old Testament with Dr. Joel LeMon. Dr. LeMon, with his signature bow ties, was one of those professors who knew how to not only give his students the material they needed but also pass on his love of the things he taught. And this man loved the Old Testament, especially the psalms. In the midst of teaching them (which took him three class periods longer than it was supposed to because LeMon thought everything was important), Dr. LeMon said something that affirmed that moment in my mother's arms: "As long as you are talking *to God* and not *about God*, you are in a faithful relationship with God and are participating in a faithful act of worship. The act of yelling at God, telling God why you are angry, of demanding that things change and change right now—the act of crying out to God, 'Why would you do this to me?'—is an act of worship." As it turns out, being angry with God is a choice, and in fact, being angry with God is far from the act of a failed person of faith; it is a vital, necessary part of a healthy and faithful relationship with God. It's an act of worship, and that act of worship is called *lament*.

Lament takes up a surprising amount of space in the Old Testament. People giving God the what for, while not taught in Sunday school, is actually almost a third of the Bible. Lamentations itself is an entire book of the Old Testament. When categorizing the psalms, experts say that 40 percent of them are psalms of lament.* Chapter 3 of Ecclesiastes reminds us that for *everything*, there is a season. A time to be sad and a time to mourn are sanctified. Yet the church, it seems, makes room only for praise: God is good all the time! All the time God is good! While that might be true, sometimes it doesn't *feel* true. Sometimes it feels like God is playing some kind of sick joke on us—and we are supposed to just smile our way through it? Seriously, God? But we aren't. God invites us to cry out to God, to be comforted by God and by one another, and to ultimately call out for change. But before any of that can happen, first we need to admit something is wrong. We need to admit that we are not OK with our lives and our surroundings. We need to lament. We must lament to God, we must lament with one another, and we must lament as a prophetic act to the world. Somewhere in our spiritual formation, lament has been lost, has been labeled unfaithful, as just some spoiled child's whining. It is not. Lament is our way to reconcile an unjust world with a God who loves us beyond all measure. Lament changes us, and it changes the world, if only we trust God enough to cry out.

* Brian Kaylor, "Sing a Song of Lament," Word & Way, January 9, 2017, https://tinyurl.com/y3873ear.

Part One

LAMENT TO GOD

1

DO GOOD CHRISTIANS
HAVE BAD FEELINGS?

An Invitation to Biblical Lament

The first time I attempted to explore lament seriously as an act and a practice, it was on a whim. In my first year of seminary, I was required to participate in contextual education. In other words, I had to learn how to be a theologian in the world, where things are messy and hard, not just to think about God in terms of the neatly defined boxes of attributes we make up in academia. My contextual education site was the largest youth prison in the state of Georgia. Once a week, three other seminarians and I presented our IDs and left our keys and cell phones at the front desk. We were then buzzed through a series of doors until we were locked inside the library, where we waited for the children to be escorted to us by guards.

Inside that severely underresourced library, we got to know the children who had been locked up by the state. As we learned their stories, one tiny piece at a time, we learned two things. First, that they always needed help, and second, that what they were given wasn't help but punishment. Every single child in that place, if you could get past the facade of toughness they were using as protection, was a kid who made poor decisions, like all kids do, and who had been failed by the adults that were supposed to protect them. There was a lot of blame flying around that place, and almost all of the blame landed on the kids.

The easiest way for them to process all this trauma was to blame themselves. The kids were often looking for someone or something to blame. Haven't we all been looking for that? It had to be someone's fault that they were in jail, and they determined that it was their fault and that they deserved what was happening to them. If they could just learn the right lesson, they would be able to earn their way out of that terrible place and move on with their lives. If they could blame themselves, they could be in charge again. This blame game was compounded by the predominant theology of the youth prison. Most of the kids were at least marginally Christian, and many of the volunteers who came in on the weekends told the kids about a God who did everything for a reason. The kids were told only of a totally benevolent God—that they were locked away from their family and friends because that somehow this was the intention of that good, loving God.

While I was learning to love a theology that considered contexts, systems, and power structures in the classroom, I also learned how much bad theology can hurt those in the prison system. Ideas about God and how God works in the world are amazing, but they have serious consequences we need to be aware of. The kids knew it was absolutely not God's fault they were in prison, and that left the idea that somehow they were in prison because God wanted them there and they deserved it. How do you talk to a God that wants you to be locked up and traumatized? How do you build a relationship with a God who is benevolent but who also put you in jail? What does it mean to a fifteen-year-old girl who is being abused by our criminal justice system that God is all-powerful when the judge who seems pretty dang powerful in her life won't even hear her case? These were the questions these children forced us to confront. I still don't have a good answer for them, but I did want to introduce them to a new way of interacting with God.

In our Old Testament class with our bow-tied professor, we learned about lament. Our group decided to try introducing this kind of prayer to the kids in the prison. We sat at the table in the poorly stocked library, and we all checked in, explaining how we were feeling and why we were experiencing those emotions. Then we told them what we would be doing for the day. We would be writing our own laments. We would be telling God how we really felt, why we were angry, how we were disappointed or scared. Mostly, the kids had a lot of questions: "What do you mean, yell at God?" "What do you mean, tell God to change what is happening to me?" They were a little afraid we were leading them into heresy. They had never heard anything like this before. Were they allowed to talk to God like that? Was anyone? I saw the question on their faces, and I totally got it. Lamenting to God was a new concept to me as well, one I wasn't totally comfortable with either, but I also knew that in the hardest parts of my teenage years, lament was what had allowed me to keep believing in God.

We went to the Bible. We checked psalm after psalm after psalm, and the kids were a little scandalized. You *were* allowed to talk to God like that. It was all over the Bible. Jesus did it too. Then we took out the paper and pencils that had been counted in through the metal detectors, and we wrote our own laments. For the first time, the girls were asking the questions they had been hiding for months. They had permission to feel the things they had been trying not to feel. They began writing down everything they had been afraid to ask. Who was going to come save them? If God was so just and benevolent, why were horrible things happening? Why did the abuses keep coming? We left the jail with no answers. But we left knowing something powerful had happened. The girls had told God the truth. They had written gorgeous and holy prose in the hardest place they had ever found themselves, and God did not strike them down. Rather than being punished by God for lamenting, the girls felt comforted. Telling the truth to God—in all its awful suffering and anger—brought relief.

God Desires Our Lament

Lamenting may seem strange to those of us raised in churches that only had prayers of praise and gratitude, but the Bible calls us to lament. It is not just that we *can* talk to God like that but that we *should*. There is a time and a place for lament. Ecclesiastes tells us this when it says there is a time for hope and despair, for work and for rest. Lament is necessary for a full relationship with God, our community, and our world. The Bible tells us that God knows us intimately, has our names written on God's palm, knows the number of hairs on our heads. We do not have to hide from the

God who knows us this closely, this minutely. We can in fact bare our souls, our deepest hurts, to God. Unfortunately, many of us were never taught how to cry out to God.

We only know how to pray in the ways we have seen other people pray. When you think about prayer, what does it sound like? It might be soft and scripted. It might be loud and demanding and victorious. It might be silent. Different traditions have very different expressions of prayer, and some of those traditions are better at embracing lament than others.

I have always been a little ecumenically promiscuous—there isn't a religious experience I am not at least a little bit curious about—and thus have encountered a large variety of prayer experiences. I have prayed with Catholics and learned how to do the rosary with a woman who was trained as a nun. I have watched as people have fallen out or were slain in the spirit, and I sometimes speak in tongues. I love a well-written liturgy, and I also freestyle from the heart. I have watched a woman weep at the prayer rail, and in that moment, it was the holiest thing I had ever seen in a church. I have sat in silence until the discomfort drifted away, and I have cozied up with God and taken a nap. All of this has brought me closer to God, and it is all prayer. But in all my experiences with prayer, only my mother and Dr. LeMon have told me lament is holy.

We have the tendency to pray in the ways that our community prays. You won't find a charismatic church in the mountains reading out of the book of common prayer. You likely won't find an Episcopal church that is expert at praise dancing. We know what we see—we learn to pray at the feet of our spiritual parents, just like we learn to talk and eat. And almost no Christian faith tradition shows us how to lament. Mostly we praise God, and then we thank God. Then we bless the congregation and walk out the door. Luckily for us who grew up without the lament tradition, the Bible gives us tons of examples of it.

While it typically isn't a part of our Christian tradition, lament is a *huge* part of the Bible. As I learned from Dr. LeMon, Lamentations is a whole book of the Bible, but most people haven't read it. Of the psalms, more than a third are classified by biblical scholars as lament psalms. For example, Psalm 102 is labeled "A prayer of an afflicted person who has grown weak and pours out a lament before the Lord." The psalm begins,

Hear my prayer, Lord;
    let my cry for help come to you.
Do not hide your face from me
    when I am in distress.
Turn your ear to me;
    when I call, answer me quickly. (Ps 102:1–2)

This is a prayer specifically for the events when we need to cry out to God. It was written for occasions when we feel totally empty and abandoned. It is designed for the times when everything is terrible. In the Old Testament, lament is deeply holy. All the prophets had seasons of lament. In fact, for most of them, lament was their main gig. Hosea describes his marriage to a prostitute and wails at the tragedy it brings him—a metaphor for what God's people were doing to God in his time. Ezekiel literally lies on his side in the middle of the town wailing. In the time of the prophets, lament was how God got the attention of God's people. Then and now, lament can be how God's people capture the heart of God. Jeremiah says that God hears our laments and responds, "Then you will call on me and come and pray to me, and I will listen to you. You will seek me and find me when you seek me with all your heart" (Jer 29:12–13). Lament is hard. Lament is gritty. Lament doesn't hold back. Lament is the truth about our hearts, about our communities, about the reality of our world and how it does not line up with how God intended the world to be.

Lament is part of a long, biblical, and holy tradition of telling God that you are not OK and that you certainly are not OK with the way the world works. Moses cries out against Pharaoh; Jesus says his piece against the Pharisees—even flipping the tables and calling the religious elite a den of thieves. Job wants to know "Why me?" and asks God that very question pretty much to God's face. Jesus talks to God like Job talked to God, demanding that this cup of suffering be removed from his hands and begging God for a different way. Jesus tells God he doesn't want to do what God is asking. I used to think that this was because he was the son of God and had some kind of special privilege that was not available to me. I am not sure how I came to that conclusion, but I was wrong. Jesus was raised in a Jewish home, with the Hebrew scriptures. He knows the psalms and lamentations.

Jesus sounds like a prophet of old not because he was born speaking like that but because he was raised with a template of how to cry out to God. He was raised to talk to God with the full range of human emotion, in anger and desperation and grief. And Jesus did exactly that. He wept and asked God to take away his suffering in the garden of Gethsemane. He wept with the sisters of Lazarus, joining their grief when their brother died. From the cross, Jesus quoted a lament psalm (Psalm 22, which is normally attributed to David, is quoted by Jesus in Matthew 27).

When You Don't Have Anything Nice to Say

I do not ever remember a time when I haven't wanted to please God. I grew up in a Christian home, the kind where you find yourself at church two or three times a week because of the various committees your parents are on. We had a key to our church hanging next to the spare set for our car. It was a major part of my childhood and my adolescence. The things I learned at McCord Road Christian Church were incredibly influential and continue to be very dear to me, but there was a glaring hole in my Christian education. No one taught me how to give God my big feelings.

No one told me how to handle my anger in Sunday school. We didn't talk much about sadness either, or annoyance. We didn't talk about what to do when you felt hopeless or disappointed. We talked about how there was always hope because God would make a way and that since God knows the desires of your heart, disappointment was only temporary. That our behavior should reflect those beliefs. Rage, blinding frustration at the injustice of it all, was not something that was ever explored, even though I felt it. Whether explicitly or not, I learned that big, ugly feelings toward God and God's plan in my life were off the table for faithful believers—especially for faithful female believers. Girls were allowed to be appropriately sad, but anger or real, deep grief was too unbecoming. I never saw anyone's face contort in rage or turn bright red as they fought hot tears during prayer time—well, anyone's but mine. As far as I could tell, these big feelings weren't a problem for anyone else. It seemed that other Christians didn't have the sorts of feelings I did. Or at least they were better at not talking about them. I couldn't figure out if I was broken, or if they were lying, or if I just . . . had bigger feelings than most people.

I have never, ever been accused of hiding what I feel. From infancy to today, what I feel is what you see. If you flip through the stacks of picture albums at my mother's house, there are family pictures where I am laughing hysterically, overjoyed by the doll buggy I was gifted or a chance to be at the beach, and just as many where I am clearly furious. More than one Easter dinner or Christmas Eve photo has my sisters on one side of my dad beaming, while I am on the other side, red faced, teeth gritted, arms across my chest. I am pretty sure my dad is being used as a barrier so no one participating in the photo gets hurt physically (since it is pretty clear my feelings are already hurt). I had to learn to make my overly expressive face work for me. Despite my best efforts, I was never able to hide it, so I just started telling God what I really think.

If we believe in an all-powerful, all-knowing God, doesn't that God know what we're thinking? We might as well say it too, then. Shockingly, I've found that God agrees. Sometimes I raise my eyebrows at God when I don't understand, asking, "Are we really doing this?" And God responds, "Oh, you think you can do better?" I felt like this when I was asked to go to seminary, a career move right when my husband was leaving grad school and my youngest was entering prekindergarten, because didn't God know our lives were supposed to get easier? I don't know exactly how I have come to this arrangement where I speak however I want to God, but it has been happening for a while. It works for me. The more I talk to people about this quirk and the more I pray in public, the more I realize how scandalized people are by my propensity to tell God exactly what I actually think (as if God didn't know already!). My prayer requests have raised more than one eyebrow in small groups. Apparently, not everyone cries and uses the word *bullshit* when discussing their life predicaments. Apparently, not everyone in the mom's group admits that there are certain ages that are just desperately hard. I have, on more than one occasion, been asked if I could answer my own prayers by simply feeling less, as though I hadn't spent most of my twenties trying to do just that with abysmal results. What else is there to say sometimes except *"Seriously, God?"* Sometimes you have to tell God what you really think, and what you really think is "If this is some kind of joke, God, you are not funny."

I like to say that God and I have worked out a deal. I speak to God any kind of way, and God certainly returns the favor. I spent some time in my early thirties begging God for a sign about whether or not to switch churches, and right when I was sure God was ignoring me, what I now call my home church installed an actual literal sign that I could not miss: "Eastside Church: Creative, Historic, Inclusive." It was everything I was looking for. It was all the things I had been praying for. I would not have changed anything had I designed it for myself. I remember yelling, "Oh! You think you are so funny!" I'm pretty sure God responded, "Actually, I am hilarious."

Do Good Christians Hide Their Feelings?

Telling God what we really think is, for many of us, the exact opposite of what we have been doing in church. In church, we slap a smile on and wear the mask I have heard called "church face." As in, "I was crying in the parking lot, but I put my church face on and walked into the foyer and told everyone I was fine." We are taught that being happy and joyous honors God, and it does if you are actually happy and joyous. But if you aren't happy and joyous, not telling the truth doesn't do yourself or your community or God any favors. God doesn't need us to protect God's image, and God doesn't need a cheerleader. God needs people who live authentic lives, and that means experiencing the full range of human experience *with* God, not in spite of or away from God. That means crying when we are sad and not putting on our church face when we are angry or disappointed. It means saying, "I am not OK, and I do not know if I am going to be OK" because it is true, even if you are expected to say "fine."

As I mentioned earlier, I am cursed—or blessed, I suppose—with the inability and complete lack of desire to ever put on a church face, especially in church. With parents who served as elders and trustees, the anchor of the alto section of the choir, and the leader of the longest-running Bible study, I had little choice but to make myself at home in the church building. The first public fit I can remember throwing was in church. I think I was six years old. My sense of justice was offended when I was, according to my own assessments, asked one too many times to give up something I wanted. I reacted by sitting in the middle of the room and screaming until my mom picked me up by my elbows and carried me out to the minivan where I could calm down.

To my mother's delight—or chagrin, depending on the day—I didn't necessarily grow out of this strong sense of justice. When I was fifteen, my sister and I got into a yelling match in the church narthex between the two Christmas Eve services. She accused me of embarrassing her in front of a boy. I accused her of being something you aren't really supposed to shout at your sister in the narthex on the eve of baby Jesus's birthday. We were both supposed to sing in the choir. I didn't make it to the second service; I was crying in the pastor's office instead. Since then, my sense of justice has matured, as have I, and I now tend to open my mouth and get carried away when I think other people are being unfairly treated too, not just me.

While I am not proud of upsetting my mom or missing the choir performance, I can say with certainty that I have a long track record of abandoning my church face. Even when my mouth doesn't say what I am thinking, my face always does. Our bodies often tell us how we feel before our brains catch up. It is just that some of us are better at hiding it than others. But here's the thing: I don't think that hiding is serving us. It is, in fact, hurting us. We need to be able to vocalize when people are being unfairly treated or when we are hurting. The place for that should be in prayer. The place for that should be in how we talk to God. The place for that should be the church.

Somehow, we've decided that church is where everyone is supposed to be OK, fine, great! We are afraid our church family can't handle our sorrows. Perhaps we are afraid God can't handle the hardest stuff in our lives. Somehow we have decided that how much suffering we have to endure is in direct relation to how much we have missed the mark with our Christian God. We may say we believe in grace and abundant opportunity, but the way we tend to hide our suffering shows that we think that how sanctified we are and how "fine" we are just might be correlated. In a world where every good thing is evidence of being blessed (there's a hashtag for that), we push down the suffering and smile through our pain. After all, God doesn't give bad gifts, right?

We Can't Fix What We Don't Acknowledge

Somehow we have internalized that being a Christian and leading a Christian life means we will end up with less pain, less suffering, less bad stuff happening. When that doesn't turn out to be true, we double down. There are so many cheesy Christian sayings that get flung around out of context and often can be boiled down to "stop whining": God will make a way when there seems to be no way! God doesn't always show up when you want God, but God always shows up right on time! We tell everyone, maybe especially ourselves, that what we are going through isn't that bad—or, if it is, that it must somehow be good for us. I do believe that God will eventually make good out of all the horrible things that happen in this world, but that doesn't make it any better in the moment. In the moment, it still totally sucks. Once, while expressing the frustration of having my teens and twenties be plagued with chronic illness, I was told that I should be grateful for my suffering because God handcrafted it just for me. That's right: God *handcrafted* an unexplainable autoimmune disorder that left me in pretty much constant pain and then *gifted it to me* because God loves me. There apparently was not a gift receipt. I for sure tried to return that gift. Statements like this depict a terrible God.

Sentiments that turn God into an abuser and a gaslighter are in exact opposition to what Jesus came for. Jesus said he came for the sick, not the well. Jesus came in solidarity with our suffering—to perfect it or allow it to change us and our world, not to erase it. We need God because this world is desperately broken. If you've lived more than ten years (or maybe even if you haven't), you certainly have experienced a piece of that. Yet we tend to keep the fact that we are hurting away from God. Imagine going to see your doctor, but instead of explaining what is wrong with you, you immediately tell the doctor you are fine or that it isn't that bad. Why even bother going? Do you even believe that doctor could help? The doctor can't treat a pain she does not know about. She can't treat a pain she hasn't been told the truth about. If you keep telling her that your broken foot is fine, the doctor may not take X-rays. She wouldn't bother treating a foot that isn't hurting. We don't behave like that. It would be absolutely ridiculous, and we know it. But this is how we often come to God.

Coming to God and to the greater body of Christ as though everything is fine when it is not fine is exactly what we do at church. Then we wonder why church doesn't feel good or why we can't heal. You cannot heal a wound you ignore. You can only make it worse, and sometimes permanent. Even if we can't tell anyone else (and I hope you have people in your life you can let it all hang out with), I hope you are able to tell God what God already knows anyway: how you really feel. God wants us to come just as we are—weary, exhausted, burnt out, and sick. When we show up raw, when we lament, Jesus shows up with us. Jesus comes for the weary and the broken and hangs out with those who are lowly. If you are that, if you are feeling those things, then perhaps you are closer to God than you have ever been. In order for this truth to sink in, we have to first acknowledge the weariness. We need to admit to our own suffering, to our shortcomings, to our own humanity.

Not talking about our hardships doesn't lessen them or make them smaller. Instead, pretending we are fine often complicates and compounds our grief. I have news that is not news: Everyone is going to die, and all of us in the meantime will have terrible weeks or even months. Some of us will have whole years that we wish we could be erased forever. For something that is actually guaranteed to happen to us, we sure spend almost no time talking about death and grief. No one wants to talk about suffering, about palliative care, about dying well and grieving well and mourning well. But if we don't talk about those things, we don't do those things. We don't express our loss, and we don't tell people how we wish that things were not like they are. We do not admit that we are having a hard time or that we simply do not want to go on. We end up pretending that everything is fine until the hardship is far away and we don't have to talk about it. This doesn't fix anything, so it seems like we might be better off choosing something else. There is a better way. Lament creates a space where we can name the things that are broken in our lives and invite God and our community to enter into the work of healing those wounds with us.

We cannot ignore hardships and hope they will go unnoticed. When my kids were toddlers, I learned it was really important to tell your babies you are coming back. There is even an episode of *Daniel Tiger's Neighborhood* with a song I used to sing about how I would come back to them. I would stand at the door putting my coat on and finding my keys while singing the promise "Grown-ups Come Back." The instinct of the parent is to just disappear to the grocery store or to the coffee shop or to work. We think the kids won't notice and we won't have to deal with the meltdown. That . . . never works. What the child actually learns from this behavior is you may disappear at any moment with no explanation. This makes them clingy and anxious. You go to the grocery store for seven minutes of peace once a week if you are lucky. But if you haven't taught your kids how to deal with that, or even name the abandonment they feel, your seven minutes of peace might become to them a nightmare.

We do the same thing with death. We don't talk about it. We pretend it isn't happening. And we do the same thing with disappointments, with breakups with friends or partners or churches, and it all hurts. We graduate, we move on, we get married and change the family structure forever. All that is OK; some of it is even good. All of it is part of the reality of living. And also all of these changes can be really, really sad. We need to tell someone how we really feel or we will end up scared and clingy and horrified that the good stuff is going to disappear when we aren't looking. Acknowledging our grief is the only way to process it. God invites us to let God into our grief with us. God wants to hold our hands while we cry.

Blessed Are Those Who Mourn

I don't know who decided that holy people don't suffer. It must have been someone who wasn't very close to God. Jesus lived in a lot of pain, and Mary had to watch her son die. His death was prophesied to her while she was still breastfeeding, but that part—the part where a mother gives birth with an intimate knowledge of her son's death—doesn't make it into the Christmas pageant. Maybe it should. Maybe there should be a Hannah who sees Mary and Jesus and says those things about the mother being pierced all the way through because she would watch her son be pierced all the way through. I long to be in a church that tells the truth about suffering and frustration right from the beginning.

We are allowed to bring our broken bits to God. We are allowed to talk to God like we are working out our relationship, with all the ups and downs and hard times. We don't have to always be happy; we don't have to always look on the bright side. God does not and will never ask that of us. We can fight it out with God, and yes, we can even be angry at God. The Bible leaves a lot of space to lament—and not just in a soft and delicate way.

We are allowed to talk to God like that. Lament is the stuff we say to God that isn't praise or gratitude. It is the stuff we say to God when every-thing is too hard, when we think God's "plan" for our lives is terrible, when we think God is either cruel or an idiot. It is the stuff we say when we experience a tiny misfortune on the way to a huge one, like a flat tire on the way to a funeral.

My friend grew up in a house where you weren't allowed to say that you were sick, only that you were fighting sickness. You were not allowed to admit that it really was as bad as it was because, in James 3:6, life and death are said to be in the power of the tongue, and her family took that literally. Your words became your reality, so saying anything negative at all means manifesting that reality, they thought. While I certainly believe that there is power in our words, I don't think there is a simple straight line between our words and our circumstances. Bad things do happen, people do get really sick, and we get sad and disappointed even if we never talk about it. Life really can be completely unfair and miserable. Ignoring the reality of the darkness of our world doesn't make those bad feelings go away.

This way of believing may seem extreme, but it is baked into almost every part of American Christianity, whether we know it or not. There is a part of Christianity commonly known as the prosperity gospel. Basically, it is the idea that God wants us to prosper physically, socially, financially, and so on. If you are not prospering in these ways, then you need to figure out how to please God again. While many of us pooh-pooh the idea that we could believe such a superstitious thing, if you have a faith shaped at all in America, some prosperity doctrine has probably leaked in. But the prosperity gospel is a lie. It is decidedly unbiblical. Job did nothing wrong and had horrible things happen to him. Moses told God, "No!" and God worked with that. Moses often asked God, "Why me?" and yet God continued to ask Moses to lead. You are absolutely allowed to tell God how bad life is at the moment and how hard it is to slog through it. Lament doesn't further cement your existence in misery; rather, it allows you to be honest with God about how you feel. Lament provides a path through the suffering, and it allows you to get to the other side.

Lamenting Is Holy: The Bible Tells Me So

If you think that telling off God is for only the holiest among us, let me direct your attention to David—a liar and a cheat, a rapist and a murderer. He is, in many respects, the absolute worse. I wouldn't want to be friends

with him, and I certainly would not choose him for spiritual leadership
(or any kind of leadership). But David wrote psalms of lament, and God
did not turn him away. I find it ironic that some of our best laments in the
Christian tradition come from the lips of a man who caused so much pain
in so many people's lives. But it gives me a small comfort to know that no
one earns their right to lament. We don't have to be mostly good, or even one
little bit good, to tell God when we are miserable. It is our right to lament
because God gives that right to us out of God's deep and abiding love, no
matter who we are or what we've done. It is our job as much as worship is.
It is in fact an act of worship to cry out in anger, in frustration, in sorrow.
God doesn't expect us to have a stiff upper lip. Instead, God invites us to
complain, to whine, to lament.

Just look at the psalm Jesus chose to quote from the cross, Psalm 22,
which goes like this:

> For the director of music. To the tune of "The Doe of the
> Morning." A psalm of David.

> My God, my God, why have you forsaken me?
> > Why are you so far from saving me,
> > so far from my cries of anguish?
> My God, I cry out by day, but you do not answer,
> > by night, but I find no rest.
> Yet you are enthroned as the Holy One;
> > you are the one Israel praises.
> In you our ancestors put their trust;
> > they trusted and you delivered them.
> To you they cried out and were saved;
> > in you they trusted and were not put to shame.
> But I am a worm and not a man,
> > scorned by everyone, despised by the people.
> All who see me mock me;
> > they hurl insults, shaking their heads.
> "He trusts in the Lord," they say,
> > "let the Lord rescue him.

Let him deliver him,
    since he delights in him."
Yet you brought me out of the womb;
    you made me trust in you, even at my mother's breast.
From birth I was cast on you;
    from my mother's womb you have been my God.
Do not be far from me,
    for trouble is near
    and there is no one to help.
Many bulls surround me;
    strong bulls of Bashan encircle me.
Roaring lions that tear their prey
    open their mouths wide against me.
I am poured out like water,
    and all my bones are out of joint.
My heart has turned to wax;
    it has melted within me.
My mouth is dried up like a potsherd,
    and my tongue sticks to the roof of my mouth;
    you lay me in the dust of death.
Dogs surround me,
    a pack of villains encircles me;
    they pierce my hands and my feet.
All my bones are on display;
    people stare and gloat over me.
They divide my clothes among them
    and cast lots for my garment.
But you, Lord, do not be far from me.
    You are my strength; come quickly to help me.
Deliver me from the sword,
    my precious life from the power of the dogs.
Rescue me from the mouth of the lions;
    save me from the horns of the wild oxen.
I will declare your name to my people;
    in the assembly I will praise you.

You who fear the Lord, praise him!
All you descendants of Jacob, honor him!
Revere him, all you descendants of Israel!
For he has not despised or scorned
    the suffering of the afflicted one;
he has not hidden his face from him
    but has listened to his cry for help.
From you comes the theme of my praise in the great assembly;
    before those who fear you I will fulfill my vows.
The poor will eat and be satisfied;
    those who seek the Lord will praise him—
may your hearts live forever!
All the ends of the earth
    will remember and turn to the Lord,
and all the families of the nations
    will bow down before him,
for dominion belongs to the Lord
    and he rules over the nations.
All the rich of the earth will feast and worship;
    all who go down to the dust will kneel before him—
those who cannot keep themselves alive.
Posterity will serve him;
    future generations will be told about the Lord.
They will proclaim his righteousness,
    declaring to a people yet unborn:
He has done it!

David is in a seriously bad spot in this one. I don't know which one of his escapades is going wrong, but he might actually die. He is sure that God does not hear him. His heart feels like melted wax. All his bones are out of joint. He is a despised worm. If you think teen pop songs can lean too heavily on hyperbole, I suggest you see your way back to the psalms. David isn't just saying "I feel like this, but I know my feelings are nothing compared to you" or "I am fighting feeling this with the power of God." No, David is saying this is absolutely how it is: "I am abandoned. I am defiled." Most importantly, David is saying all these things to God as an act of worship and prayer. Jesus then echoes them at the moment of his terrible death. This, my friends, is lament.

Practice Makes (Im)Perfect

The Bible says that we don't have to feel good to be in right relationship with God. We don't have to only say nice things. We only have to tell God the truth. As we think about healing and expanding our faith, it is important to practice it. Practice gives us the space to try something out—even be bad at it for a little bit. When we practice lament, we learn to relate to God in a new way. Writing our own laments is a helpful exercise as we began to explore new ways of speaking to God.

First, take a moment to reflect. Was there a time in your life when you did not understand why God was not intervening? Is that time now? Maybe it was a long time ago, or maybe it is a really fresh wound. Second, use the template below, which comes from David's lament in Psalms 22, as a way to construct your own lament toward God.

I do not by any means want you to use this template as some kind of rigid checklist. Don't think, *Oh! I should lament, so here I go*, and then follow these five easy steps. There is quite enough scripted, infomercial-style theology to go around. Don't feel like this template is the only way to lament; it's simply an example of how to get started. Writing lament is less like classical music, with its perfect notes played the same way every time, and more like jazz. I don't know exactly what is going to come out, but I do know my audience and the key I am in, and that can make truly beautiful prayers.

There are five parts to a lament psalm, with examples from Psalm 22:

1. The introductory cry ("My God, my God, why have you forsaken me?" [Ps 22:1]): The practice of naming your circumstances, your sorrow, and your misery is the first part of any lament psalm.

2. The lament proper ("My God, I cry out by day, but you do not answer, by night, but I find no rest." [Ps 22:2]): This is the part where you let God totally have it. This is what some Christians might call whining.

It is certainly not the way my Sunday school taught me to pray. But here it is: where you tell God how hard everything is, let God know exactly how you are feeling, and lay it all out.

3. The confession of truth ("Yet you brought me out of the womb; you made me trust in you, even at my mother's breast. From birth I was cast on you; from my mother's womb you have been my God." [Ps 22:9–10]): It may seem slightly incongruous to hail the beauty and power of God here, but it's actually the reason that Christians pray to God in the first place. We believe that God can do something about our suffering and our problems. We believe that God has done wonderful things for other people, has saved them from the very trials we are going through, and frankly, this is why we are pissed that God hasn't shown up for us yet. Some say this is the part where we remind God who God is and what God has promised to do with us, God's people. It doesn't make any sense that God is all-knowing and all-powerful and also good and *also* that the world is messy and horrible. This is the place for us to hold both of those things.

4. The petition ("Deliver me from the sword, my precious life from the power of the dogs. Rescue me from the mouth of the lions; save me from the horns of the wild oxen." [Ps 22:20–21]): This is where you are invited to tell God exactly what you want. Do you know? Do you know how you want God to move? Can you imagine a new way forward? If you can't, that is OK. I think, "God, can you freaking do something?" Is a perfect petition and it is the one that I use probably most often.

5. The motivation ("I will declare your name to my people; in the assembly I will praise you." [Ps 22:22]): This is an if-then statement. This section surprised me the most when I first learned about lament psalms. I had been told you couldn't bargain with God, and maybe that isn't exactly what you are doing here, but it certainly seems like it. This is where you tell God why you should be saved.

6. The vow of praise ("Posterity will serve him; future generations will be told about the Lord. They will proclaim his righteousness, declaring to a people yet unborn: He has done it!" [Ps 22:30–31]): Finally, if this thing pans out, do you promise to praise God forever? Will you

tell the world? Will you put it all over Facebook? If it doesn't work out, what will your response be?

Imagining a Different Way

I believe that each of the laments you give to God is treasured by God. Lament is a deep gift in a relationship and is always holy ground. This work of lament is not easy and may feel strange. Even if they fit, new ways often feel awkward at first. It does not mean they are wrong. As you explore lamenting to God as a personal practice, I pray that you are comforted. May the outpouring of your grief be accompanied by the outpouring of God's love. May you work through the practice with patience and mercy for yourself and your circumstances. May your wounds be covered in balm. May you be close to God.

2

WHAT IF I AM NOT FINE?

Learning to Feel All Our Feelings

top me if you have heard this one before: Someone is in the middle of telling you why they are having a really hard time. You think they are done, but they aren't. It isn't just that they had a baby three days ago and are still wearing adult diapers and can't sit because of the stitches. No, that isn't hard enough; in addition to all that, their toilet exploded, or they found bedbugs in their mattress, or their roof collapsed and they have to stay in a motel—with a baby—while they leak from every orifice and their spouse goes to work, leaving them alone to keep their toddler from killing the new baby. You are gobsmacked by how hard that sounds. You are astounded that everyone is alive and clothed. And in the middle of this hard and horrible story, the person this is happening to sucks all the tears up, smiles, and says, "But I know I am really lucky. I have a beautiful new baby, and the insurance covers the mess, and my spouse has a job to go to, and I get to be the mama of these little guys." They have stopped crying, and they are smiling, but the gratitude hasn't reached all the way to their eyes. They are still exhausted.

This has played out before my eyes so many times. In the midst of telling me how hard everything is, people stop themselves to let me know that they know how good they have it and how truly grateful they are. I know why they do this; they have been trained to do this by the times before when they were trying to tell someone how hard something was and they were interrupted with "but at least you still have . . . ," "but you should be grateful for . . . ," or "but think of all the people who have it worse . . ." They were interrupted so often, they now do it themselves. They downplay their pain. They remember to be grateful. They assure us it isn't that bad.

Sometimes it is that bad. We don't have to be grateful for our pain. We do not have to be fine. In fact, saying we are fine when we are not and telling ourselves it isn't that bad hurts us. It has very real consequences emotionally, mentally, physically, and spiritually. Instead of being "fine" and keeping a stiff upper lip, God asks us to be honest with ourselves and with God through the holy act of lament. God is not the one asking us to be fine.

From infancy, some of us have been praised for our sunny disposition. You've heard it before in phrases like these: "She is such a happy little girl," "He gets over disappointment so quickly," and on and on. But emotions like fear, anger, and sadness aren't bad. They just are. Emotional responses of all kinds are part of the reality of being a human being. Bad things happen. Our lives get hard. We are just plain worn out some days. It is simply the reality of being human that things are gonna suck a little bit some days. Life is hard and complicated, and you can be happy and very sad at the same time. You can be grateful that you have a home you love and not at all grateful for the dishes that keep showing up in the sink when you feed people. You can be so proud of your lanky ten-year-old and mourn the squishy toddler she will never be again. Your joy at the good does not invalidate your sadness or anger at the bad. Emotions are weird. They don't happen in a straight orderly line; they're more like the scribbles of an abstract art piece no one understands. Grief is obvious sometimes, but it often shows up in the weirdest places. That is allowed. God isn't asking you to be OK all the time.

I was shocked to find my grief waiting for me when I was about to get married. The date was set for New Year's Eve, and the Christmas before, I couldn't stop crying. I knew this was the last Christmas morning I would be spending with my parents, as next year I would be with my own little family. It was the last time I would not have to split time and manage schedules. Of course I wanted to get married; of course I wanted to start a life with my new husband. But also it felt like the final kiss goodbye to my childhood. Every Hallmark commercial had me all sniffly. I attempted to hide it, but then my face would turn bright red and I'd do that weird extraloud gulp thing. I wish I hadn't been caught off guard by this grief. Of course I was sad; things were changing and change is hard. Being sad that my time with just my original family was over didn't mean I wasn't thrilled to be getting married. It just meant something I loved was coming to an end.

Change is pretty much the only constant in our lives. Maybe that is why every single state I have lived in has that terrible joke about how if you don't like the weather, wait five minutes. Sometimes the change is more than welcome, but sometimes it really is hard. Grief is the price we pay when we love someone, when we love something, when we have fully embodied and embraced a season and are sad to see it go. It is important to acknowledge that grief. It is necessary if we want to also fully embrace the next season.

When I was pregnant with my second baby, I found myself totally surprised by my own grief. My girls came pretty close together age-wise, and I remember being sad in my third trimester with my second daughter that our tiny family of three was about to change. My sixteen-month-old was about to be the big girl, not the baby. As the youngest of three, I knew how special the sister relationship could be but also how sometimes that meant keeping secrets from your mom. My oldest hadn't even been alive two years, and I was about to totally change her life. Was I sad that I was pregnant? No. I was thrilled to raise sisters, but change, even good change, means that we won't have the thing we have now anymore, and that is sad. We need to let ourselves be sad, even if we are grateful, even if someone else has it worse. Lament can help us fully embody that heartache and prepare to embrace the next season. Feelings are messy, and that is OK.

Holding It in and Harming Ourselves

The effects of putting on our church face and insisting that we are fine take a real toll on our bodies. Negative emotions have consequences, whether we deal with them or not. Consciously or unconsciously, we find coping mechanisms. Instead of working through our grief and telling God why things are not OK, we numb it. We overeat or starve ourselves. We watch entire seasons of this year's feel-good documentary on Netflix. We drink too much. We withdraw from things and relationships that matter to us.

We stop caring. We do whatever we can to avoid the pain, and when we run out of those coping mechanisms, the pain is still there.

To me, nothing exemplifies the propensity to numb the feelings rather than address the issues more than becoming a mother. Mothering is hard, but I've learned that you are only supposed to say that if you also say how grateful and satisfied you are with your children. This leads to something I call "wine-mom culture." Wine-mom culture is the pervasive attitude that you and your kids are doing great while also joking (but not really) about how much wine you need to get through the day. You aren't allowed to have any negative feelings, but you are allowed to drink them away. Wine-mom culture comes out of a refusal to feel our own feelings. Being a mom is complicated and deeply personal. There are things you have to give up, there are a lot of expectations placed on you, there is a lot you are navigating, and whatever you do, don't forget that you are supposed to love it all. If motherhood is next to godliness (it isn't) and you are bored out of your skull or find your three-year-old's tantrums particularly hard to deal with—well, that isn't allowed.

I have found the hard way that these feelings aren't always appreciated. Once, I was pretty much at the end of my rope and escaped to my friend's house. She had invited some people over to make essential oil rollers. As we worked, she asked what things our kids struggled with so that she could suggest various oils for our ailments. I guess I was supposed to say that they needed help sleeping or sometimes had a tummy ache. Instead, I blurted out, "Do you have anything that can make a three-year-old less of an asshole?" Whoops. She didn't. There was a lot of sympathy, but I certainly made it awkward with my transparent comment.

Instead of being truthful about how every single moment of our lives is not treasurable (because when we are, things get awkward), we drink and then joke about our sorrows so we feel less alone. But sometimes three-year-olds are jerks, and being bested by a tiny human day after day is the absolute worst. Responding to these challenges by not dealing with our problems is so prevalent there are multiple wine labels called things like "Mommy's Time-Out," "Mommy Juice," and so on. That is a sign that something is seriously wrong! We should be able to say that things suck without hiding behind numbing jokes. The experience of my child screaming on the floor of the Target because I will not let her lick the shelves is not a moment I will be treasuring, and drinking "Mommy Juice" is not going to help me deal with my anger and stress.

Not dealing with our trauma also has physical consequences that scientists have been able to measure. We hold our emotional pain in our bodies. Our buried anger turns into high blood pressure. Our body changes the way it works because it assumes we are always in danger. After all, we got all worked up, but we never let it go, so we are telling our bodies they still need to be afraid.

The frontal lobe is the part of the brain that regulates emotions and helps us make decisions. Frontal lobes, and their size, help explain why teenagers who seem extremely smart often make such boneheaded decisions: they don't have fully developed frontal lobes, which means that they physically cannot process all the risks of the situations they put themselves in. Here's the other thing: frontal lobes shrink when we have unprocessed trauma, and this shrinking affects our emotions and decisions. When we don't release how we feel, it literally becomes a physical part of us. While we believe avoiding lament will keep us far from the bad things of this world, it actually makes the bad things a permanent part of us. We become worse at basic functioning and being able to make decisions in the future when we are not honest about our sorrows right now.

Lament allows us to move forward. By connecting with our feelings and working through them with the God who created the systems we have and the emotions we were designed to feel, we are able to leave the trauma behind and move on in wholeness. The world is broken, but we are good; God tells us so. When we interact with things that tell us the opposite, we must work through them. That takes work. It takes time. It takes intentionality. There is no class in college on how to feel your feelings. Most of us don't know how to do it. We have to practice. We have to give ourselves the opportunity to lament, even if we do it poorly at first.

God Isn't Asking Us to Be OK

This year, for Lent, I abandoned all the giving up. Instead, I actually told people how I was every time they asked, "How are you today?" The first discovery I made was that I spend most of my days not knowing how I am. When someone asked me, "How are you?" I had to figure it out. If you ask me what I have done and what is still on my to-do list, I can rattle off all the items. If you ask how I am, I can maybe remember whether I have eaten. But my emotional state very often gets neglected. I have kids and a job and a whole little church to think about. Who has time to know how they are?

Lent had not even started yet when someone on the internet heard I was thinking about this attempt to know how I am most days. I was immediately told that this was a truly selfish practice, that keeping track of how I am feeling is somehow not hard work and is also not good for those around me or even marginally better even for myself, and that it wasn't a sacrifice and so couldn't be a Lenten practice. He had one thing right: this was not a sacrifice. Sometimes God does ask us to sacrifice, but more often, God calls us into wholeness. This was an exercise in wholeness, and it wasn't selfish. Instead, it was a holy practice to allow me to better connect with myself and therefore be more honest with God and those around me. Being our whole selves is a gift to the world, even when it is a snotty, tear-stained, messy gift. It isn't selfish to know yourself, and self-knowledge is a vital part of being whole with God. Further, this practice proved to be far from selfish because it blessed others by giving them permission to be real with themselves around me.

I wonder if the man who told me how selfish it was to check in with myself has ever done the work of knowing what he feels or has ever been with those who are emotionally mature enough to know what they are feeling. This kind of self-awareness is incredibly hard work. Those of us who have been around emotionally mature and integrated people know how hard they work at it and how welcoming their vulnerability can be. In my experience, when I do awkwardly blurt out how I actually am to some poor unsuspecting soul, they very often return the favor. When my mask cracks, so does theirs.

During a Lenten season a few years ago, I attended a church full of people who insisted they were fine. Meanwhile, I wept through the service every week. I couldn't even tell you exactly why; it was almost as though the only time I had to catch up with myself was there, in the pews. Sometimes

I could make it all the way through the worship and the sermon, but Communion always did me in. I would walk to the front and stand in line with my face bright red and dripping. I counted myself lucky if I wasn't making weird snuffly puppy noises while I cried. For a long time, I wondered if everyone around me noticed and thought I was a weirdo (at best) or that I was being inappropriate. Mostly, no one noticed. It turns out, other people are thinking about themselves as much as I am thinking about myself. But a funny thing started happening when people did notice. They would text me that they were sad too. They would ask me quietly if I was ever mad at God. They wanted to know what I did with all these big feelings of mine. They thanked me for being real. It turns out that feeling my feelings wasn't a selfish act; it was a gift of freedom to those around me. Me feeling my feelings gave them room to feel theirs.

In a society that tells us those with the least amount of problems are the holiest, the most blessed, it is so common for us to hide our sorrow. There is some unwritten rule that expressing any emotion other than joy and gratitude is whining and complaining. That we should just suck it up, buttercup. We shouldn't. It isn't holy to hold church face, and you aren't closer to God when you have fewer problems. We need to practice telling the truth to ourselves so that we can tell the truth to our community. We need to abandon the lie that the luckiest among us are the holiest and stop pretending to be sorrowless.

Who Has the Time to Cry?

One of the reasons we don't lament is because we don't know we need to. We stuff ourselves full of things to do, and then, caught up in the work we've created, we don't need to know how we are. We live in a world where being busy is a badge of honor. I know almost no one who isn't legitimately busy. In intercultural studies, the United States typifies what is called a Doing Culture (as opposed to a Being Culture). Living in America means having a lot to do, a lot to care for, a lot to think about, a lot to handle. Having all these things to manage means that we often forget to manage our feelings. We don't rest, so we never have the space to realize that we need to lament. Here's the thing, though: Rest isn't something we have to earn. As human beings, we have a right to rest, to process, to become self-aware, and to lament.

One of the most profound thinkers on rest is Tricia Hersey, creator of the Atlanta Nap Ministries. She builds public places specifically for Black bodies to utilize for rest. In a culture built on the labor of Black bodies, believing that Black bodies are fully human and entitled to rest is revolutionary. Rest, she says, is the way we remember we are good and that our bodies are good. She encourages not thinking of it as some kind of reward we get when we do "enough" work. We should rest because we are human and our bodies deserve it. Just as food shouldn't be given or withheld based on what we do and do not do, neither should rest. Rest doesn't just mean sleep (although that is seriously healing and can often help us become aware of how we feel). I am talking about all kinds of rest. We often don't know how to do things that don't produce other things: to sit, to meditate, to sabbath. We don't know how to sit still long enough to tune into the things we might need to lament.

During seminary, I was asked to pick up a different prayer practice every two weeks and reflect on it. The one practice that was the most powerful for me was silence. Silence gave me the space to know what I was feeling. It gave me the space to claim other feelings instead of being too busy for them. It let me think about how I felt about my position in the world. I practiced silence in the car. I was by myself, and I had no radio, no NPR, no music. Nothing. It was awkward at first, maybe even a little scary, but eventually (barring horrible traffic), my breath would slow a little and I could connect with myself. And only then was I able to connect with God. I cleared out the noise and noticed the things the Holy Spirit was asking me to attend to. The Holy Spirit asks us to pay attention to things at the very core of who we are: our mind, our body, our heart, our soul. Together, these elements of humanity make up the sum total of who we are. Keeping them compartmentalized doesn't do us any favors. Whatever we are hiding from is still there. But we don't have to face it alone; God is big enough to handle it.

Where Can We Bring Our Whole Selves?

The church should be a place where you can bring your mess, where all your humanity is embraced and affirmed. I have often heard worship leaders say from the stage that God wants everything; that God wants our whole selves. In their felt hats with their earnest upheld hands, they implore us to bring it *all* to the feet of Jesus. I wonder what would happen if I responded by running to the front of the church and letting loose the string of curses in my heart. Would they still implore me to bring all of me? They might not, but God would. God does want us to bring our whole selves to our church and to our communities. If we are to praise God with our *whole selves*, that means acknowledging our disappointments and hardships. But that's not what we do. Instead of bringing our whole selves, we have made the church the place where we praise God by plastering a smile on our faces, like that will somehow fake God out. We need to remember that praise and worship can be more than adoration. Pretending that everything is OK before God isn't holy, and it isn't fooling God.

When we are taught that having a relationship with God means only being pleased, it causes us to shut off the parts of ourselves that are hurting. We hide them behind our backs, telling our God and our friends that we are "fine." This is not what God wants. It honors God when we choose to tell the truth, to show up and say, "I am exhausted and this life feels impossible." We owe God the truth, and we owe each other the truth. I for sure don't want to go somewhere every single week where I have to be fine when I am not. I don't want to be in relationship with people who only let me see the surface. I can get that pretty much anywhere else in my life. Hell, I don't even have to leave my couch thanks to the advent of social media, with all its filters. Our churches shouldn't look like our Instagram feeds. If the church says that we believe that God made humans and called us very good, then it must displease God when we ignore half (or more) of the moments and emotions that make up the human experience. Not honoring ourselves by ignoring the pieces that are hard or the ones we don't think others will like does nothing to honor God. Honoring our whole selves, which include all of our experiences, is a better way of honoring God.

God made us with a full spectrum of feelings and a huge variety of ways we express them and even when and how we process them. I am a pretty quick processor. My husband is not. By the time he knows what he is feeling, I have moved through about seven emotions. That is fine. Both ways are good. Processing our feelings is allowed to take that long. It is allowed to hit us instantly. It's the same with lament, the holy act of expressing our pain, suffering, anger, and disdain to God. There is no wrong or right way to lament, as long as we are doing it when it is needed, honoring God and ourselves through this ancient form of worship. When we bury our lament, we stunt our own spiritual growth. We lose the ability to move forward. And we pass that on to the next generation. We need to learn to lament so that we—and the generations that follow us—can experience God more fully, deepening and growing our relationships with the one who created us to feel joy and anger, happiness and grief, peace and frustration.

Feeling Our Feelings and Knowing Our Selves

For lots of us, there is a litmus test for public displays of emotion. If someone dies or if someone is getting a divorce, then you can cry in public. Men in our society are allowed to show extreme anger or extreme joy while watching sports, but only then. But sometimes it is just the ordinary stuff that puts us over the edge, and that kind of grief and sadness needs to be allowed too.

I like to say that when it comes to my daughters and me, our feelings come in one size: extra large. In fact, at the end of a vacation, when the excitement of a piñata on a beach was simply too much to bear, my three-year-old daughter started crying. All the adults on the beach sprang into action restuffing the broken piñata and attempting to make everything better. But Priscilla didn't really need everything to be better. She didn't need anything fixed; she just needed to cry. Yes, she was disappointed she did not break the piñata, and yes, she was preemptively afraid that she would not get enough candy (she was with her grandparents; she did not need to worry about that), but really she was just exhausted by the week of family fun. Finally, surrounded by adults, she looked me dead in the face and choked out between sobs, "I'm just having a hard *tiiiiiiiime*."

Sometimes we are just having a hard time. It is all just too much. We are just too tired, there was too much excitement, and we are having a hard time. But we don't welcome those feelings in ourselves. We tell ourselves we have to suck it up and be grateful. Priscilla was grateful for her time at the lake with her cousins and the piñata and the fireworks to come. Also, it was all too much, and she needed to be comforted. Both of those things were true, and given the space to process that anxiety, she was able to move forward. I wish I gave myself the kind of freedom I give my children to just have a hard time, to lament about the things that are small but also are the things we are crying about.

No one is going to come out of this life unscathed. That is a promise, friends. Even Jesus was resurrected with scars. So we might as well let ourselves tell each other when we are just having a hard time. Maybe there doesn't need to be a reason. Maybe we just are. As her mom, I was able to simply comfort my little girl in her purple swimsuit with the fancy tutu. I was able to gather her in my arms and rock her back and forth and whisper, "Shh, shh, shh, shh, shhhhhh" rhythmically into her head. She didn't need anyone to fix it. She wasn't even really sure what needed to be fixed. But she knew enough to know she was having a hard time. She just needed someone to be there with her in the midst of her hard time. At the end of this, when she was calmed down, my nineteen-year-old cousin looked at me. "Wow," he said, "it is great that she knows to say that. Sometimes I am just having a hard time too. Good job."

Embracing Your Feelings Is Holy: The Bible Tells Me So

It is easy to underestimate just how powerful knowing and saying how you are can be. Name the feeling and cry your way through it (or shout, or cuss, or punch things that aren't alive and won't scare anyone). It won't change your circumstances, but it will change your soul. Expressing your reality, especially to God, makes it so you aren't alone in it anymore. It has been this way forever—so long, in fact, that it happens in the first story of the naming of God. That story comes from the book of Genesis, and its heroine is a woman named Hagar:

Now Sarai, Abram's wife, had borne him no children. But she had an Egyptian slave named Hagar; so she said to Abram, "The Lord has kept me from having children. Go, sleep with my slave; perhaps I can build a family through her."

Abram agreed to what Sarai said. So after Abram had been living in Canaan ten years, Sarai his wife took her Egyptian slave Hagar and gave her to her husband to be his wife. He slept with Hagar, and she conceived.

When she knew she was pregnant, she began to despise her mistress. Then Sarai said to Abram, "You are responsible for the wrong I am suffering. I put my slave in your arms, and now that she knows she is pregnant, she despises me. May the Lord judge between you and me."

"Your slave is in your hands," Abram said. "Do with her whatever you think best." Then Sarai mistreated Hagar; so she fled from her.

The angel of the Lord found Hagar near a spring in the desert; it was the spring that is beside the road to Shur. And he said, "Hagar, slave of Sarai, where have you come from, and where are you going?"

"I'm running away from my mistress Sarai," she answered.

Then the angel of the Lord told her, "Go back to your mistress and submit to her." The angel added, "I will increase your descendants so much that they will be too numerous to count."

The angel of the Lord also said to her:

"You are now pregnant
    and you will give birth to a son.
You shall name him Ishmael,
    for the Lord has heard of your misery.
He will be a wild donkey of a man;
    his hand will be against everyone
    and everyone's hand against him,
and he will live in hostility
    toward all his brothers."

She gave this name to the Lord who spoke to her: "You are the God who sees me," for she said, "I have now seen the One who sees me." (Gen 16:1–13)

Hagar gets a really terrible deal in this whole setup. She is younger, she is a foreigner, she is a slave. We don't know whether or not she wants to be a part of this plot, but I very much doubt it. I wonder if she herself even registers her own desires in this situation. What difference would it make? She has no choice in this matter. No power in her own life. Hagar does as she's told. And it works. But I can't imagine that she thought she would be punished for doing her duty. She is carrying a child, as she was essentially commanded to do, and then she is hated for it—so much so that she decides running into the desert, where there is no food or water or shelter guaranteed, is her best option. She has never been this vulnerable before.

Then God shows up, the God of Abram and Sarai, the ones who got her into this situation in the first place. It must have felt impossible to trust that God. God shows up wanting to know why she is in the middle of the desert when it is *God's* people who drove her to this desperate act. God has a lot to say to Hagar. God promises so much to this woman who has nothing, who is sort of expecting, or maybe even hoping, to die in the desert. God gives Hagar so much hope for her future and the future of her son, and then she faces God and names God "El Roi," which means "The God who sees me." Abram and Sarai see Hagar as nothing more than a prop in their plan to outsmart God, and then Sarai sees Hagar as a reminder that Sarai was being failed by God. Abram, meanwhile, just wants to make it all go away. But El Roi truly sees Hagar.

God does not need us to ignore our problems in order to bring about good things from our suffering. God can see them. We don't need to run off, and we don't need someone to ignore the problem. We don't have to hide from God. Our most powerful moments are when God sees us. But we have to let God see us. We have to be aware that God already knows all the things we are attempting to hide, and we have to choose to share those things with him (in an angry voice or a despairing voice or a frustrated voice or whatever type of voice we have). By allowing God to see our pain, we can experience this God who sees. Our pain is not silent. Our pain is not invisible. Even if the rest of our community refuses to see our pain, God sees it.

Practice Makes (Im)Perfect

Lament isn't something we only do with our minds; it is also something we do with our bodies. I find that healing can often mean looking at who you used to be. Some people call it reparenting, or parenting themselves. I call it being kind to your inner toddler.

What are some ways that you've used to express hard feelings? I was a literal throw-myself-on-the-ground kind of person. My face turned red. I yelled. Even now, there are occasions when I still need to do this. Pain, anger, and frustration pretty much just live in my body, even when I think I am over it. My inner toddler needs to let them out. Here are my two suggestions: (1) Throw and break things. (2) Scream and burn things. This is not hyperbole. Literally break something or burn it. Physically get out those feelings of anger frustration and disappointment.

The first time I tried these things, I was with a group of women who had just been through some shit. Some serious shit. So I headed to the thrift store and bought all the plates I could find. Then, after checking with my friend who is much better than I am about having plans that keep everyone safe, we lined up and chucked ceramic plates as hard as we could at the wall outside. We were at an Airbnb at the time, and I am sure the neighbors were wondering if they should call the police. But we desperately needed the release. It was interesting to see how differently some of us expressed this cathartic release of lament. I raged and threw. Another woman seethed quietly, looked steadily, and shattered her plate with precision. Others seemed sort of catatonic until the plate they threw shattered. Then they started weeping. It is hard to describe how good the physical representation of our pain felt. We already knew we were angry or sad or frustrated or brokenhearted, but our bodies didn't know what to do with our emotions. We gave them something to do, something we could experience. We could feel our hands releasing the plates and see the glass shatter. We could hear the ways the plates cracked and watch the pieces fall to the ground. Maybe the most important thing is that we stood and cheered for one another. We supported that release of grief instead of shutting it down. Some of the women needed to see those of us already predisposed to feel our feelings do it first so they knew they could. For others, acting angry unlocked the actual anger they had pushed deep down.

If breaking plates sounds just too big and wild, I recommend a bonfire. Especially if you feel like you need to write things that you don't want anyone else to see, ripping and burning is a quieter practice that might not alert the neighbors to how you are feeling if you aren't quite ready to let them know. Tell your kids you are having s'mores if you need to, but take a list of grievances and turn them to smoke. While the kids in your life run around hopped up on marshmallows and Hershey bars, watch the smoke rise to God and imagine God receiving it, like God is listening to your really angry voice mail. A much smaller version of this is a candle. Light it and burn a piece of paper over your sink.

Prayer

Grief and lament are going to feel weird and foreign, but they also might feel right, like putting on a dress in a new cut and finding that it really flatters you. You may be surprised by the way movements make you feel a certain way or even remember an emotion. As you move into these practices, may you find ones that work for you. God, as we move unafraid into our grief, remind us that you are with us, that you see all of us. May we feel seen and heard in our pain, may we be able to move through trauma, and may we have the time and space in our lives to lament to a God who loves all of us.

3

CAN GOD HANDLE ALL OF ME?

Lament to a Trustworthy God

Imagine a relationship with someone you always have to be OK with, can never be mad at—someone with whom you can never express your hurt or anger. No, really, imagine for a second that you are in a relationship with someone you are totally sure loves you. Imagine this person has a lot of sway over how your life operates. This isn't a brand-new relationship. This is someone you claim to have known for years, and yet you have never ever told this person one thing that they have done that makes you angry, or annoyed, or irritated. You don't think you are allowed to say anything when this person does something that you don't like. You don't think you are allowed to be frustrated with this person.

Most of us don't have to imagine being in an interpersonal relationship with a person who we can't push back on because most of us have been there. We've wound up hiding our own selves, constantly worried about how the other person would react. It has turned us into people who constantly police ourselves and walk on eggshells. The relationship eventually became strained, and usually, one way or another, we left it behind.

You can see where I'm headed with this, and you might be thinking, "But Abby, our relationship with God is so different! God is perfect. God isn't annoying." I guess, but we are human, and so we are imperfect. I do not care how perfect you know God is in your head; we are going to be annoyed with God sometimes. Our relationship with God is human because we are humans. God isn't displeased by our humanity. God made us purposefully, with a full range of emotion. We are going to be angry. We are sure we are being dealt a raw deal. Even if you believe that God doesn't intervene . . . most of us believe God *could* intervene. This paradoxical belief makes it even more infuriating when God does not just do something already.

I know that God isn't a magic genie, but sometimes I am furious that God isn't available to come at my beckoning. Surely God could help a girl out, just this once! How dare God not work in a way that makes sense to me! How dare God let bad things happen! How dare God let horrible tragedies happen to the people I love most in this world! None of this is sarcastic. Of course we have angry, impossible questions for God sometimes, especially if God is important to us. Meanwhile, we are told we can't tell God just how infuriating God's ways are out of some sort of deference or respect. We can't let God have it. We can't be disappointed with God. We can't be human.

We actually can be all those things with God. God is big enough to handle our whole, unruly selves. God knows how frustrated we are even when we don't want to tell God, which is all the more reason we need to just lament already. There comes a point in every new relationship when the couple fights. They just do; whether it's a romantic relationship or a friendship, inevitably conflict arises. All relationships go through a first disappointment or some sort of tiff. What happens after the fight—the end of the first fight, the working through it and moving on—is a major milestone in many relationships. The relationships in which we do not care enough to engage on this level are the ones that get left behind. We just give the relationship up.

Some of us don't know if God can be trusted after we have it out with God because we've never tried it. We claim to be in a relationship with Jesus, but we are too afraid to fight with him. Maybe we are afraid to be in conflict with God because we think that all conflict has a winner and a loser, and we're scared that we will lose. But God isn't interested in besting us. God longs for an authentic relationship with each of us, and that means (at least in my case) occasionally fielding our asshole remarks about what God *should* be *doing*. God is big enough to handle that. If we're going to be in relationship with God, we have to express all we feel. Otherwise, we're essentially giving up, letting God know it isn't worth it to us.

Avoidance Is Not a Permanent Solution

My husband is a rhetoric professor. My youngest calls it being a doctor of ideas. He is a literal expert at argumentation. Yes, that is annoying sometimes. No, he doesn't win all our fights. He also teaches interpersonal communication and how to get along in a group. The other day we were discussing conflict-management styles, and we got to avoidance (as an enneagram 9, I think he might know something about avoidance). He said this: "If there is avoidance happening, then the conflict is already fully in play."

Avoidance doesn't mean that there is no conflict. It just means that someone is choosing to engage in the conflict by pretending it doesn't exist. If the way your roommate leaves the dishes in the sink for three days makes you angry and you stop going into the kitchen for a week at a time, the conflict still exists. You might not be yelling, but the frustration and distance are present. The dishes conflict is still there. Many, or most, of us have convinced ourselves that as long as we don't engage in our conflicts with God, then we don't have a problem with God. False. When we avoid a conflict, it means we have already engaged in it. Continuing to avoid it just means the conflict gets stuck in perpetuity.

For people you are only going to know for a few weeks, avoidance may be the best strategy, but if we want to have a relationship with God forever, then we need to choose a different one. We have to engage actively. Engaging God in conflict may seem scary, I know. But here's the thing: God already knows our pain and invites us to treat God like the doting mother hen God promises to be. We can trust God with our lament. God wants us to engage with God.

God Can Take It

I know that it seems like we are supposed to be happy as much as possible and avoid "bad feelings" so we do not become ourselves "bad" or a "burden." But the Bible tells us that God values all of our emotions. Psalm 56:8 even depicts God collecting our tears in a bottle in a lot of translations. Assigning feelings a negative value is actually complete and utter trash, meant to control us. Feelings aren't naturally bad or good. They just are. They just . . . are.

This is good news for me. We have already established my (perhaps accurate) reputation for being a fit-thrower as a child. If I felt like things were unfair or I was not being heard, there was nothing that would stop me from ensuring I at least got my say (though, thanks to good parenting, not often my way.) As an adult, I still have a burning desire for justice, but I am often afraid I am still just "throwing a fit." This fear has led to many attempts to tamp it all down, to control my feelings and push them away. Once, I was clearly trying to minimize my enormous disappointment when a friend asked me why I was doing that. I thought about it and said, "I guess I am afraid you would think I was throwing a fit." She looked at me and said, "So? Fits are fine. They happen." So what if you throw a fit? Throw it! God can take it. Being happy, sad, angry—those things are allowed. Hurting people because you feel these things is not allowed, but the feelings themselves are, which is good because they show up anyway. God can handle our complicated feelings even when no one else can. We do not have to be afraid God will abandon us in the midst of our sorrow. Rather, we can relax knowing that God is close to the brokenhearted, that God values our tears, treasures them, just as God treasures us.

We are not God, and we do not have the mind of God, and that means that sometimes we think that what God does totally sucks. We think God's so-called plan that we see developing in our lives or the lives of those around us is the worst idea ever. As the card that Emily McDowell sells says, "If this is all in God's plans, then God is terrible at planning." It is OK to think that. Even Jesus asked God for a different way.

Anger in the Hands of a Healing God

Even when things aren't terrible and sad, we can still have a need for lament in our lives. At twenty-six, I experienced a miraculous healing, but years later, I still needed to lament the pain from my illness. I didn't owe God pure joy for my healing, and God didn't expect or ask that of me. Healing is so strange and complicated. It is beautiful, and it can also be really heavy. So many of our biggest joys are also folded into complicated losses. I know because I have experienced a miracle. I got mysteriously ill when I was thirteen. I had mono, but never fully recovered. I got better and then worse. I was tired almost all the time. I missed a lot of school. I just didn't feel good. But I looked fine. The doctors tested everything. I had an ultrasound on my heart to make sure it was pumping blood appropriately. I was checked for hyperthyroidism. I was checked for anemia. I was checked for Lyme disease. I was checked for depression (and I was depressed, but probably because I was a teenager with a mystery disease). Finally, at seventeen, we had an answer: I was diagnosed with fibromyalgia. In that moment, a diagnosis felt as good as a miracle. It sort of was a miracle. At last, I was believed. I was seen.

It was such a relief to be seen by a doctor who believed me. Fibromyalgia. My suffering had a name, and we had a plan. I went off sugar and preservatives (goodbye, Taco Bell). I drank so much water. I got special dispensation from the doctors to go to the bathroom without a hall pass. And I learned to live in chronic pain for another nine years. I got married and had to sit down in the middle of the photo shoot. I started working and sometimes threw up in the hallway from the pain. I went to church and sat on a yoga mat. And then . . . I was healed.

There is and there isn't more to it than that. Don't get me wrong, I was, and am, grateful to have experienced a miraculous healing, but after I was healed, I didn't know I was allowed to have complicated feelings rather than just walking around leaping and praising God. I thought that my recovery required that I turn in any right to lament. Sick people were allowed to lament; healed people should be grateful.

It wasn't until years later that I realized how alone I had felt, realized how sad I was that I had gone through my teens and most of my twenties with a body that ached all the time. How there were things that could have been different, could have been better. I didn't know I was allowed to tell God, "Thanks for the healing, but couldn't it have been eight years earlier? If you could do it now, why not sooner? Wouldn't it have made just as good a testimony for me to suffer six months rather than thirteen years?"

I don't have answers surrounding the whys and hows of suffering. I have thoughts and ideas and, most of all, a lot of empathy. Anyone who professes to have all the answers about God and suffering is not telling the whole truth. But I do know that holding back from telling God how I really felt made me wary of trusting God at all. It all came to a head again when a teenager I knew came down with fibromyalgia. I felt like I had been betrayed all over again: God hadn't spared me, and now God was not sparing another child. I felt lost, alone, and unseen all over again. I avoided talking to God because I didn't know how. Here's the thing, though: Avoidance didn't make any of the suffering or any of my feelings go away. It just made them harder to live with.

Finally, I told God all about it. I told God that I was angry, that I had felt abandoned, that I was grieved over the loss of a prom and a wedding and a honeymoon and a college career without daily pain and random days I couldn't get out of bed. I wept for the experiences that I did not get to have and the ways that things had to be different. I yelled at God the same way my sister yelled at the anesthesiologist who showed up ten minutes past the closing window for her epidural: "You were late!"

And God could totally handle it. God could handle the anger and the sadness. God did not punish me for these feelings. I was not put on the naughty list, and my healing was not revoked (I mean, I didn't earn it, so I suppose doing something I did wrong would not mean it'd get taken away). Instead, I was met with an overwhelming sense of empathy—a sense that *of course* I felt that way, *of course* I was angry, *of course* I was sad. I felt God weeping with me. And it was enough. God doesn't need to be protected from our feelings. God isn't fragile or far away from us. God already knows, so we may as well tell God. We are allowed to be in an honest relationship with God. Our anger, our sadness, our frustration won't scare God from us. God isn't judging us for the way we feel.

Conflict in the Body of Christ

Christians who claim to be in relationship with God but always insist they are fine lead to much larger dysfunctional patterns. If we can't learn to bring God our grievances while still believing God loves us, it becomes impossible for us to be in conflict with other human beings and still want the best outcome for everyone. I wonder sometimes if the church, by giving the people of God the impression that they cannot be in conflict with God, has as a result never learned how to deal with conflict within its body.

I am not throwing stones here. As a United Methodist in the year 2020, I am just holding my breath until the church splits. Like many denominations before us, we are split on whether queer people can be ordained. Our fight has been public and ugly. I am left wondering if we can work it out amicably or if it will be a bloody mess. I wonder if anyone or anything will make it out unscathed. We don't know how to disagree with one another and are causing so much additional pain because we haven't learned the value of conflict in the safety of an all-loving God. In other words, avoiding lament (or conflict with God) leaves us unable to handle it well among ourselves. And when that happens, the church, the individuals in it, and the individuals outside of it all suffer.

So often, the church is the last group of people you feel like you can be in conflict with. I have heard horror stories of half a church leaving because of a fight over carpets. I personally have been on the receiving end of an angry phone call about the flooring. The church's inability to handle conflict keeps people from God. After all, if you can't engage in conflict well with the people who are claiming to be the hands and feet of Jesus, why would you think that you can with Jesus himself? When we hide our hurts from one another and from God, we teach the next generation to do the same. This stunts everyone's spiritual growth. If we walk with God throughout our lives, we will likely have conflict with God. We need to tell God that and let his steadfast love show us how to handle it with one another—with love, not hate.

Heartbreak and New Hope

Facebook reminded me that two years ago on this day, I was preaching for the first time at my first appointment as a pastor in my first church, New Hope United Methodist Church. The room was pretty full, which isn't hard when there are only sixteen pews in the whole place. But still, preaching to a full house was pretty great. I had a lot of dreams for that tiny sanctuary, and I could not wait to hear the dreams of the community. Both the congregation and I felt a lot of trepidation but also a lot of hope. This thing could be anything. It was a bit of a shock the next week to find that normal Sunday attendance was fewer than ten people (if you did not include my

family). It became clear that this church needed more maintenance than
I had originally thought. It was time to either shut down or rethink the
whole church. We voted unanimously to try something new.

That summer, we decided to shut down to attempt this transforma-
tion. We painted the sanctuary walls a new color and ripped up the shag
carpeting, which revealed gorgeous hardwood floors. We threw parties and
invited neighbors to join us on the lawn. We handed out five hundred
postcards and hired someone to brand our website. We took on a try-
everything, no-stone-unturned, follow-advice-from-all-the-experts approach.
Every week, we prayed together that we would have a greater impact on the
neighborhood, and every week, the same twelve, then ten, then eight people
showed up.

Nothing worked. We could get people to come to community events,
but not on Sundays. We tried cutting corners and renting out our sanctuary for music video shoots. We never really could get the finances to match
the dreams. Two years after my first sermon, I had to tell the church that
we would be shutting down. There was no response. The congregation
told me everything was fine. God was in control, and surely God would not
close the doors.

Week after week, I went to the church to preach and pastor the community. Every week, they told me they were fine. They didn't want to pray for
the church. They didn't want to talk to God about it. Everything was fine,
this congregation told me as their time in their beloved sanctuary came to
an end. If you ask me, pretending things are fine did not make the closing
easier on anyone. Avoidance made it harder.

I was not grieving quietly in these weeks. I did not think everything was
fine. I was furious. I felt like God had asked me to do an impossible task
and then wouldn't help me make it happen. I told God this, and rather than
facing silence and blame, I felt comforted. God honored my faithfulness
and the faithfulness of this congregation. Even though I did not hear God
tell me how to fix the hurt, God was near me in this time. I longed for the
congregation to have the same experience. It very well may be that they
were doing this without me, but communally, they wouldn't face their hurt
over how God had not shown up in the ways they expected God to show
up. There were just forced smiles and pain in their eyes. Endings are so

hard and complicated. Grief is always a journey. In the end, this church was going to close whether we talked to God about it or not. We can invite God to join us on our journey, but we need to trust that God can handle our lament.

Talking Back to God Is Holy: The Bible Tells Me So

Lamenting does not hurt our relationship with God or make God move away somehow. We never ever have to risk God rejecting us. If there is *anyone* in this world we can safely be in conflict with, it is God. We can push back on God. Scripturally, there is evidence that we can make our cases fervently to God: David, Elijah, Jesus, Hannah, Nathan, Ruth—all these people beg and demand things of God. They yell at God. They teach us to push back on our circumstances and maybe even get a little mouthy.

The story in the life of Jesus that shocks me the most is the one where he calls a woman a dog. I don't think I had ever heard it until I got my MDiv; it's not the kind of story that comes up in Sunday school. Most pastors avoid preaching it. We find it in the book of Matthew, and I want to share it with you:

The Faith of a Canaanite Woman

Leaving that place, Jesus withdrew to the region of Tyre and Sidon. A Canaanite woman from that vicinity came to him, crying out, "Lord, Son of David, have mercy on me! My daughter is demon-possessed and suffering terribly."

Jesus did not answer a word. So his disciples came to him and urged him, "Send her away, for she keeps crying out after us."

He answered, "I was sent only to the lost sheep of Israel."

The woman came and knelt before him. "Lord, help me!" she said.

He replied, "It is not right to take the children's bread and toss it to the dogs."

"Yes it is, Lord," she said. "Even the dogs eat the crumbs that fall from their master's table."

Then Jesus said to her, "Woman, you have great faith! Your
request is granted." And her daughter was healed at that moment.
(Matt 15:21–28)

In twenty-first-century American culture, desperation is not a good look.
We are never supposed to want anything too badly. We are never supposed
to be desperate. But this woman? She is desperate. She is so desperate, in
fact, that she bothers the people who are hanging out with Jesus. She pesters
them so much that the disciples ask Jesus to send her away. They are really
annoyed by this woman and her daughter and her suffering.

I often worry that my coming to God will annoy God and that I might
get on God's nerves. There is still some part of me that worries that God is
much too busy for my problems. Sometimes we do not say anything, even
to God, because we don't want to come off as desperate. One of my friends
is a labor and delivery nurse, and she's told me about women who don't
say anything. They are in labor, a process the Bible associates with people
crying out in pain. These women don't do that. Instead, they suffer silently
and sometimes give so little warning that there is barely time to catch the
baby! People are being paid to help these women, but they still don't cry
out, even in labor. We have been conditioned to believe that not asking
for help is always the best route, and that is simply not true.

We don't want to need anything. But we do need things. We do need
help, and we are in pain sometimes. It is acceptable to call out to God, even
if it annoys other worshippers, even if other people find it unacceptable.
You are allowed to sit and cry during a praise song. You are allowed to
tell your small group that you think what God is putting you through is
bullshit. "Screw it all" can be a whole prayer.

In this text, with this woman, even Jesus argues that her behavior is out
of line. The woman is not a part of the group that Jesus came to preach
to. She isn't an Israelite. She is a Canaanite woman (in Matthew, anyway;
she is identified as a Syrophoenician woman in Mark). She is very much
not from any tribe of Israel, and she is certainly a gentile. Who is she to
even approach Jesus, let alone demand something from him? But she has
no other options. She's desperate. So she makes herself a nuisance and
makes Jesus notice her. He sends her away, or at least he tries to dismiss
her. Actually, Jesus calls her a dog. Nevertheless, she persists.

Her demands and repeated insistence on being heard are remarkable. So many times when we hear no, we respond with "Oh, OK," instead of "Listen to me." If you're a woman, you especially cannot be too demanding. Women of color especially are simply not allowed to have any feelings. When I lose my mind over an injustice, I hear it called "a concern." When my Black friends express their concerns, they're immediately told to calm down. When I had major beef with my kids' principal, I went to the news and was called brave. My Black single mom friend wasn't even allowed into a meeting with the principal. She was "too angry."

I can only imagine how many times the woman talking to Jesus has been told to stop being so angry and settle down. In the world we live in, the more privilege we possess, the more demands we are allowed to have. The same must have held true for this woman, and she's at the bottom of the ladder. She isn't supposed to be talking to any Israelite man, let alone a rabbi with a whole group following him around. It seems that the disciples know this too. They respond to her pleas, "Ugh, Jesus, can you please get rid of this girl? She is bothering us!" Even Jesus tries to brush her off, but she is not having it. When the man she knows she needs compares her to a dog, she doesn't even flinch. Instead, she has a quick response: "Don't the dogs sometimes get a crumb?" It seems that God does appreciate a quick-witted reply, despite what I was told in my middle school youth group. Jesus hears this woman out and grants her request. Not because of her good behavior and her perfect appearance and the way she asks nicely. She doesn't have or do any of those things. Her request is granted because she comes with everything she has to demand a better world for her daughter.

I wonder if this is why they never taught me this story in Sunday school. You can't just go around telling kids (especially young girls) that you get to talk back to Jesus. They might think they can push against all authority! Even the patriarchy! As a person who is both giving the kids' lesson and also listening to her own children say who knows what during kids' time, I understand why this one might not make it in. But imagine a Sunday school classroom where we taught kids to talk back to Jesus. Our churches would be radically different if they were full of people who were raised to snap back when they really needed something from God. I am sure that a worship service full of God's children who have been taught to feel safe enough to shout at God might be chaotic, but I am also sure it would be holy ground. Prayer time might last most of the service some weeks. Our prayers would likely not be so full of hedging and filler words if we learned to approach God the same way this woman approached Jesus.

The woman demands to be heard. I can just imagine her saying to Jesus, "Look, if you are going to call me a dog, the least you could do is treat me like one. All I am asking is for you to heal my daughter." Then Jesus does. Jesus *changes his mind*. Not because someone was kind and nice enough, not because someone asked in the right tone, but because she demanded it! She would not go away. She would not take no for answer. I mean, seriously, are we allowed to talk to God like that? I don't know that I ever have. But here, the Son of man responds to it. The thing about Matthew is, the book doesn't spend a lot of time telling you *why*. We don't really know why Jesus changes his mind and then does as this woman asks. Does he realize he was sort of rude to her? Does he just want her to go away? Was it because she had challenged Jesus in front of his friends? (Please, *please* do not tell me that Jesus had a fragile ego; I couldn't take it.) I don't know. But I do know that Jesus responds to her and her bold proclamation. It's about time we all start making more bold proclamations.

Practice Makes (Im)Perfect

At the height of the blogging world's prominence, writing an open letter was the thing to do. I did it a time or two (they are on my website, but boy are they embarrassing). I wrote one to some women I respected when I felt like my faith was crumbling (Sarah Bessey actually wrote me back and I cried like a baby). Others wrote open letters to call out people who expressed bad theology against women. Outrage is total clickbait in our society, and I understand why. It feels good to get outraged. It feels good to see that other people are furious too. It feels good to know that you aren't the only angry one. It feels good to be mad at *something* when you just low key have some rage.

So with that in mind, I suggest you write an open letter to God. What can you not take anymore? What feels so unfair? How exhausted and angry are you? Tell God, and then email it to me. I'm serious. I would love to see all our laments out in the air. I don't think these letters will solve anything, but I am sure they will make us feel less alone. Lament has a way of doing that. I'll get us started. Here's an open letter I wrote to God:

An open letter to God while in a global pandemic (written in May 2020, when I thought it couldn't get worse)

Dear God,

This is bullshit. Utter trash. Are you seriously telling me there is an epidemic that is *worldwide*? Worldwide? You couldn't get a handle on it? You couldn't maybe sort of limit the spread to a single continent? You had to pick all of them? OK, so maybe you didn't pick all of them, but you could certainly save one of them, any one! Europe? South America? Antarctica absolutely does not count. Can someone have a break (not an outbreak)? And of all the times in history to have this happen, *this* is when a pandemic occurs? When everyone in the country is already losing their minds and a germophobe who isn't great at communicating is in the White House? Awesome. Just so freaking great.

God, it isn't just the pandemic. If you gave us the pandemic, could you at least have spared us from the other crushing griefs of this world? My friend's baby niece died. My other friends are recovering from a tornado that took their home. My church is still closing, and now who knows if it will even get to have a last service. It is all just too much. I know it is a giant lie that isn't even in the Bible, but why can't that bit about God not giving us more than we can handle be true? Because, Jesus, I could really use a freaking break. But I didn't get a freaking break. Instead, I got *bedbugs*. It is some kind of sick joke to get bedbugs in the middle of not being allowed to go anywhere for six weeks! It is like . . . the absolute reverse of a miracle.

Where are you in this? Why aren't you sparing more people? Why does it all have to be so exhausting? And why do I still have to feed my kids even after all this crap I dealt with all in one day? All this grief and I still have to make dinner? Maybe that shouldn't be the thing I can't handle anymore, but it is. My increasing burnout is why I was going away for a vacation that is now canceled. That is why: I needed a break. Can I please have one of those? Where are you in this?

    Feel free to sweep up some of this trash,

Abby

Prayer

I know this can be scary. Not all of us have had a lot of practice talking back to God. As you embark on this exercise I pray that you land in the arms of a God who is good and holy and big enough to handle every single bit of your sorrow and rage. I pray that you would not be afraid of the strength of your own sorrows. I pray that you would land in strong arms.

Part Two

LAMENT IN COMMUNITY

4

WE CAN ALL BE SAD TOGETHER

Lament So We Are Not Alone

The other day, my friend discovered something about the very fancy school her child attends: The playground looks so amazing all the time because . . . the grass isn't grass. It's artificial turf. It isn't real, and that is why it looks so perfect all the time. So many of us live in church communities covered in spiritual and emotional AstroTurf. We spend a lot of time cultivating a false reality where God just rains down blessings on everyone and where even when things are hard, we still are fine. It's not that bad, after all, and God is good. Yeah, that may look great, but get close and everything is a lot pricklier than you expected.

Lament births a community of real and whole people willing to truly show up for one another. Real community will always include real lament. But often, the knee-jerk reaction in the Christian community is to fix the problems, not be with the people. In other words, lamenting in community is often the opposite of what we have been taught to do. It can feel awkward. It is exhausting. It is also what everyone in the church is called to do for one another, and when we don't lament together, we make everything that much harder.

When we don't lament, we aren't being honest about our lives. When we aren't honest about our lives, we basically advertise our AstroTurf as grass: Look! We are living our best lives! Everything is great! Our churches become an Instagram feed where only the highlights are allowed. Only the adorable babies and the cute pets show up, not the poop on the floor (from babies or pets) or sleepless nights.

As a result, we all end up getting imposter syndrome. We all slap a smile on our faces and then cry in the car or the bathroom, wondering why our lives are so broken. We're left wondering why we are the only ones who feel like this, when in fact we are *not* the only ones who feel like this. It's likely that the person sitting next to us has felt exactly how we feel at some point. They might even be feeling it right now. When we are wondering if we are broken, unable to keep our lives together, the way that everyone else appears to be doing just that only adds shame and frustration to our plates during an already difficult time.

Here is the real secret: No one has it together. Life is a disaster sometimes. Terrible things happen. We live in a broken world, and stuff is going to be hard. That isn't just my opinion; the Bible says that. The Bible says it again and again. Yet we go on acting like it isn't OK to feel that brokenness when God has shown us over and over again that feeling and expressing our brokenness, and the brokenness of the world around us, is exactly what God wants from us.

Christ, and his incarnation, is a model for meeting us in our suffering. Christ did not demand that we do better and quit whining. God came down to earth as a tiny, needy baby. A tiny needy baby of an occupied class in the midst of a pregnancy scandal. In the body of Christ—the actual literal human body—God showed up for us. God wept with us. Now, as the body of Christ, we have the responsibility and the privilege to do that for one another, to show up and say, "Wow, this looks hard. Can I sit here? Can I just sit here with you and remind you that you are not alone?"

When I suffered from fibromyalgia, there really wasn't anything anyone else could do. I was just sick sometimes, and in pain most of the time, without a real alternative. Because my disease was invisible, and there wasn't anything to do about it anyway, most people I knew ignored it, and mostly I tried to ignore it all too. But that wasn't always possible. In college, I was on the speech team, and our uniform was business professional: suits, full makeup, high heels. Wearing heels all day and walking across campuses totally exhausted my body. My senior year, after eating cheese curds for dinner in Wisconsin, my fibromyalgia acted up, and I couldn't sit up at the table anymore. I asked my coaches for the keys to go lie down in the van. They'd been my coaches for four years and trusted me, so they nodded, handed me the keys, and asked if I needed someone to go with me. I shook my head and walked out to the van exhausted. I cried in the dark. Moments later, the door opened and one of my teammates crawled into the seat behind me.

"I am OK," I said through exhausted tears.

"I know," he said. "I just wanted to come sit with you. I didn't want you to be alone." *I didn't want you to be alone . . .* He saw me, knew me; he noticed me, and he didn't want me to be alone. So he came out to sit with me and be with me while I was sad and hurting. In that moment, having someone see me and offer to sit with me in my pain was deeply comforting.

(Dis)Connecting the World

Our world has become increasingly connected as far as information is concerned, and yet we have never felt more alone. The internet gives us so much to be sad about, to be angry about, and to be cynical about. We can know the names of each victim of the last mass shooting. We can know the faces of the kids pulled from the earthquake. We can fight endlessly about the last freak accident and how it could *never* happen to us because we are way too careful for all of that. But even with all this access to information, there is nowhere to adequately process the pain together.

We can see everything there is to be afraid of. Thanks to the internet, we can find new reasons to be afraid every day. Now we can be totally freaked out by every bad thing that has ever happened to anyone in the history of ever. There is no way to process all this. If we want to, or even if we don't mean for it to happen but we also don't stop it, we can stay on *enraged* forever, moving from one thing to the next without any other feelings. *The world is terrible! Look at all these dumpster fires!* I get it. I have felt this way. I have a Christmas ornament of a tiny dumpster on fire to prove it. But life goes on anyway, and I am just taxiing kids around, stuck in traffic, or making dinner, and have no place to scream. I look around and it seems like everyone else is OK, like no one else even knows how hard things are, and so I just keep going on, but inside, I am totally churning.

When Michael Brown was shot dead in Ferguson, Missouri, I was teaching high school in an affluent suburb. I would go through the day reading and writing with teenagers, some of whom looked an awful lot like Michael

Brown. At night, I would scroll Twitter and Facebook and watch the protests in the city of St. Louis. I watched as people poured out their hearts and risked their lives for the sake of justice. I went through my days as best I could, but I was just so paralyzed by what was happening in St. Louis. But I had not yet engaged in any kind of community that was working toward justice. So instead of speaking out, I just walked around, scared—of what, I did not know—and incredibly isolated in that fear.

While we have more access to information than we ever have, we have less and less time for community. We have fewer local meetups and fewer shared spaces. With the internet as our meeting place, we end up grieving in these virtual circles where we are not together to hold one another, to feed one another, to simply be together. I experienced this when my cousin died in a car accident on the way to her first job after college. One of the things I remember the most during the period of grieving that followed is that my cousins and I couldn't stop touching one another. All ten of us just piled onto the futon, onto the couch; shoved ourselves in one minivan; or had our hands on one another's backs. We were all in our early twenties. It may have looked strange from the outside, but it was the comfort we needed. We needed to be reminded somehow that the rest of us were there with one another. We needed to hold hands.

I am not discounting internet community. I have some great friends whom I have never met, and I know how important it is to those who otherwise cannot leave the house to be able to have community in real time over the internet. But it is tricky and weird, and there is something missing when we cannot actually gather together. This has become very obvious to me during the COVID-19 pandemic, when church services, weddings, and game nights suddenly became online-only affairs. If my choices are my sister on Skype at Christmas or nothing, I will take Skype, but I am not going to insist that it is practically the same thing. We need community; we were built to be communal (yes, even the introverts, you all just would rather I stop talking while we are together).

Communal lament is important. But it is hard, and I think we are still as a society working out how to do that with all our new technologies. The news comes quickly, and the mourning is confusing. When Kobe Bryant died, I watched the world hear the news and attempt to lament together in real time. There was a visceral need to somehow process this together, but it was clear so many of us didn't know how to grieve. The gathering around a hashtag was not enough, but it was all we seemed to have.

There are moments when social media makes us feel like we are together, but more often than not, it makes us feel isolated. Studies show increased depression in teen girls who spend too much time on Facebook and Instagram. Watching everyone else's perfect lives makes your own feel somehow sad and pathetic. No one talks about the hard stuff until it is already patched up, and really, who can blame them? When we try to talk about the hard stuff, it all gets more challenging and complicated. People basically ask us to get over it even when we are not ready.

Seeing One Another

We do not know how to grieve together because we have not grieved together. There are cultures where people are very good at being in grief together, but Americans are terrible at lament. We want to fix it, but you can't fix things like death. It is just horrible. It is just sad. It is just tragic. The only thing we have to offer in response is our presence, and for many of us, the idea of sitting with someone else in their grief makes us itchy.

My friends who have had spouses or children die and people I know who have gone through a divorce talk about a certain phenomenon where people simply back away. Those I know who have dealt with deep grief say that this second loss is equally painful. People just disappear quietly and without fanfare when tragedy strikes. It is as though we believe that if we distance ourselves socially from the tragedy, we are less likely to catch it, or maybe we're worried that we will further burden those who are grieving. This is absolutely untrue, but it feels true, you know? It feels like we can take this preventative measure. Distancing ourselves from others' tragedy doesn't inoculate us from it; it only makes it scarier when tragedy does strike.

No one goes through life without disappointments. Recently, I had one of those. I was deferred for ordination. After three years in school and two years serving as a licensed local minister, I was told that I was absolutely qualified to pastor . . . just not yet. This is a thing that happens in the ordination process. Also, it totally sucks. Deferral is hard, no matter how you look at it. I wanted to ask my people for prayer, and so about two days after the fact, I told Facebook that I had been deferred. I am not the first person this had happened to, I won't be the last, and frankly, I didn't want to have to explain it three hundred times while people stood and looked embarrassed for having asked about it in the first place. Social media seemed like the easiest way to rip off the painful Band-Aid.

The gift I was not expecting was this: so many people told me, "Me too." A friend messaged me to say the same thing was happening to her with her PhD, and many clergywomen I respected told me they, too, had been deferred or that the people they respected most had been. The voices of my community made the shame subside and lessened the sting. Knowing I was not alone was such a gift in a painful time. Lamenting communally can allow us to grow together and help one another. It can remind us just how not-alone we are.

Do Good Christians Fail?

What was *not* helpful after I was deferred were the comments about how this was all good and part of God's plan. This wasn't all good. It sucked. It seriously put a wrench in a lot of my plans. It hurt my feelings. I didn't want to look on the bright side. I wasn't ready. It made me feel bad for feeling bad about the thing I had every right to feel bad about. Sometimes, when people get tragic news, everyone around them disappears, but sometimes, people get exactly this: platitudes and brush-offs, being told it will all work out when actually no one can make that promise. These people may not disappear on those who grieve, but they're also not grieving with them. This is not what lamenting together looks like.

Promising that everything will be OK when in fact things are not OK and we have no way of knowing what will happen in the future is spiritual gaslighting. It is dressing up Jesus in a "Good Vibes Only" T-shirt and declaring that the most spiritual people can handle anything without being sad. This is simply not true. As we've seen, it wasn't true in biblical times, and it isn't true today. You don't have to keep calm and carry on; you can be desperately sad. It is a gift to let other people be desperately sad with you and to be desperately sad with those in pain.

There has been a recent surge of research on resilience and grit. As it turns out, the best way to be good at bouncing back is to normalize failure. Communal lament leads to a much healthier community because it leads to a more resilient community. Lament teaches us how to deal with our failures, as individuals and as groups. Together, we mourn; together, we fail; and together, we find the strength to keep going.

When we only see and celebrate each other's successes, we see our failures as freaks of nature instead of just what happens sometimes. It makes us think there is something wrong with us when there isn't anything wrong with us. Our world is broken, and bad things happen. We tend to face these things alone, but we don't have to. We don't have to tell only the stories of failure that led to great successes. Because of our unwillingness to lament together, when each of us faces a major setback, we assume we are the only ones who have faced this hardship. We're left without a road map to navigate our way out of our sadness. When we lament as a community, we are blessed with a community that has already faced whatever it is we might face. We are gifted the strength to go forward.

Most businesses fail. Most start-ups are not good ideas. Most church plants don't make it. But we don't hear those stories. We don't give those people book deals. We don't make movies about people who tried something and poured their whole heart and soul into it . . . and then had it fail miserably. Those stories don't sell. Surely the market can't support anything but winners! But that isn't real. We aren't all winners. Some of us chase down our dreams only for them to disappear like dust through our fingertips. There needs to be space for that too.

We like to dissect people's failures and pinpoint the why. I understand. The autopsy gives us more answers, and the answers make us feel like next time, we will be smarter. Sometimes, this dissection can help us avoid mistakes, but more often than not, we do it so we can promise ourselves that we are different and if we just have enough information, we can avoid all the potholes and not have any of those problems. Except life doesn't work like that. Life is not a video game, and there is no manual for how to play through it with minimal damage. But we can *talk* about our failures and let people know that they are not merely the sum of their failures. Failing just happens sometimes. I can tell people that the church I love won't make it without putting all the blame on lack of effort from me or the congregation or the denomination, because those stories just aren't true. The truth is, it just didn't go our way, and that is OK and absolutely heartbreaking all at the same time.

I don't understand why it is the Christian viewpoint that we should mitigate all failure. We are the people who believe in redemption, who have our cornerstone built on resurrection. How can we have redemption if we refuse to acknowledge that a problem is a problem in the first place? If nothing dies, then nothing will be resurrected.

Feeling Alone in Church

We don't want to be alone . . . and the church is supposed to be a place where you don't have to be alone. But church can feel incredibly lonely—and it's because we do not fail and lament together. As the youngest of three daughters, I knew what going to college would be like. I wasn't afraid of it. I was ready. The first week and weekend, I was doing great. I found people to hang out with, I got along with my roommate, I got minimally lost on campus. But then Sunday came, and I walked into the church my mom attended when she was at the same college. The congregation was small, and I do not remember at all what the pastor said. I do remember how hard I cried.

I couldn't remember a time when I didn't go to church. I had never met a service I didn't love. But I had never gone to a new church by myself. I was always at my own church or tagging along with someone. I felt so alone. One stranger halfway joked about making his daughter come sit next to me. I wiped my eyes and told him I was fine. I never went back to that church. I pretty much stopped trying to go to church altogether. Being alone was too hard. I only knew church as a communal experience, and I couldn't bear the isolation.

Church *is* a communal experience. It has always been a communal experience. And lament was always supposed to be a communal experience. There are ways we can be with one another. Are you a person who is willing to be with people, even when it is hard? I know that sitting with someone while they grieve might be weird for you, but you can get used to it, and if you can't, well, even awkward things are worth doing. What is not worth doing is naming and claiming and promising God will work everything out, or disappearing from places of suffering, or letting communities remain Instagram feeds instead of places for broken people to bring all of themselves.

Holding One Another's Hope

Toxic positivity is how we most often find ourselves responding to the hard things in other peoples' lives. "Good Vibes Only" may be a cute T-shirt, but it is no way to be in community. It gets even worse when we add Jesus on top. "I know it is hard, but God will work it out" is easy for us to say, but it is a giant lie. We don't know that God will work it out. We want to believe that, but it isn't necessarily true. We can be spiritual and also desperately sad. We can be holy and cry out to God. God can love you and not heal your problem the way you want it healed. False positivity does not equal hope.

I learned this by living with fibromyalgia for thirteen years. The space between diagnosis and healing was really long. I started by being so sure God would heal me, by showing up at every healing service and believing with everything I had that it was my turn to be healed. But eventually, I couldn't do it anymore. The best thing for me to do was to go on about my life, to learn to live in pain and assume it would always be like this. I wasn't being unfaithful or unbelieving. I was simply doing what I needed to do to move on. I asked for healing, but God didn't give it to me when I wanted it.

Quietly, there were people in my life holding that hope for me. My sister just tucked my hope in her heart and carried it around. She didn't interrupt every time I cried out in pain with a prayer for healing. She didn't tell me that I needed to wake up expecting no pain. She sat with me, rubbed my back, and asked God to not forget about healing me. My dad, my mom, a friend from church—they all knew it was too much, and they respected the way I simply could not bear to think about healing right now. They held my hope for me when I could not. We are not meant to hope alone. Hope is often a burden best shared.

Slowly, the idea of healing was not too much for me to hold. The hope was not too much, and it was handed back to me. I lived in that weird balance of expectation and contentment, and when I could not, I just put the hope down. And that was OK. I am convinced that being given space to work out my wholeness while sick, without the burden of hope burning a hole in my pocket, is the very thing that allowed me to be healed.

Now I am learning to hold hope for others. When the burden of their shattered marriage, their shattered health, their shattered faith is simply too much to bear, I send an email, a Voxer, a prayer. I will hold your hope until you want to carry it again. It is OK to put it down. Hope is just too heavy sometimes.

When it is too hard to hope, that is OK; your community can hope for you. When it is too hard to believe that the light will come in the morning, you don't have to. You can have someone else hold your hope for a while. Or your faith, or your anger if you know you should be angry but are just too tired. This is why we recite the creeds together, why we take time in church to chant all at once about what we believe. We believe in the Holy Spirit. We believe in the virgin birth. It is a reminder that when all of it is too much, there are other people who can hang on. When someone else is tired, it can be your turn again, like the way the trumpet section of the marching band can hold the long note forever. Lamenting in a community gives us more space to feel whatever we need to feel, to say whatever we need to say, while other people hold our life and our society together for us. Communal lament teaches us that we don't have to hold the whole world in our hands, because God does.

Grieving with One Another Is Holy: The Bible Tells Me So

Job is the oldest book in the Bible. It tells the story of people unable to just be with their friend who is suffering. Job has a seriously bad day. Every single thing goes wrong. Everything has been taken away from him, and he has done absolutely nothing to deserve it. There is little comfort in dissecting Job's story. The only thing he has done is be a righteous man and because of his goodness, he's chosen for a sick contest between Satan and God that results in Job losing all the things he has and most of the people who matter to him, not to mention his health. I have read this story so many times, and yet I still have no defense for what God is doing. But Satan, I understand.

Satan strikes a deal with God. He gets God to agree to allow Satan to test Job, and suddenly horrible things start happening to Job: "The Lord said to

Satan, 'Very well, then, everything he has is in your power, but on the man himself do not lay a finger.' Then Satan went out from the presence of the Lord" (Job 1:12). Interestingly, the label the story uses to describe Satan is "the accuser." In a finger-pointing, gotcha world, I think we need to spend a long time with the idea that Satan is first named as "the accuser." Satan, the embodiment of evil, the antithesis to God's love, shows up first as a blamer, as the spirit of "What did you do to make this happen?" When we don't make room for lament in our communities, the default is to accuse: "Surely you could have avoided this if only you had been better."

Job's friends do the right thing initially. They spend a long time just sitting with him: "When Job's three friends, Eliphaz the Temanite, Bildad the Shuhite and Zophar the Naamathite, heard about all the troubles that had come upon him, they set out from their homes and met together by agreement to go and sympathize with him and comfort him. When they saw him from a distance, they could hardly recognize him; they began to weep aloud, and they tore their robes and sprinkled dust on their heads. Then they sat on the ground with him for seven days and seven nights" (Job 2:11–13).

No one said a word to him because they saw how great his suffering was. But then, they start talking. The fourth chapter of the book of Job is a diatribe by one of Job's friends about how surely Job has brought this onto himself. I think it is easy to blame the friends, but this is often our initial reaction too: to say something. This is a terrible instinct. Someone recently told me, regarding pastoral care and chaplaincy work, that when you sit with someone who is in need of spiritual care, whoever talks the most is the one being cared for. When you are sitting in the midst of another's pain, you aren't in a position to point fingers. It isn't enough to be around someone who is suffering; physical proximity doesn't cut it. We are called to be with them, to be present with them. God asks us for solidarity when we're among those who suffer.

We need to be able to just sit, and be, and listen if we are going to care for one another as we are asked to. One of my dearest friendships was solidified by simply sitting, listening, and being present in a hospital room. Megan and I weren't sure we were best friends until she got devastatingly sick. During her hospital stay, she didn't want anyone in the hospital but her wife . . . and me. I would bring my guitar and play it poorly and just sit there. She didn't need small talk, and she didn't need me to explain anything. She just needed someone she trusted to be there. She just needed not to be alone.

Practice Makes (Im)Perfect

In order for us to be able to lament well with one another, we need to be able to say what we want or need, or that we don't know what those things are yet. This part is really hard. We are trained to minimize our pain and not be a burden to anyone else. But being in the church means carrying one another's burdens! We are supposed to need help. God designed us to give and receive help. Needing other people is a feature of community, not a flaw.

I have some friends who have been through some serious shit. They have been with me as I have been through some shit. We have developed a kind of shorthand. Here are the rules for our language of need: You are always allowed to be not OK. You are always allowed to be so sad you can't function. Often, we say, "Do you know what you need?" If we are on the "need help" end, we are allowed to say, "I can't choose; please just handle it," or "I just need you to sit with me," or "I cannot cook one more thing; can you order my family a pizza?" This doesn't have to be only for things like death or divorce. You are allowed to crumble because it is Tuesday and life is hard.

A corner of my life crumbled, and it wasn't something that you get a meal train for, you know? It wasn't a death or a birth or a sickness. It was more of a personal heartbreak, but it totally wrecked me. My friend Angela, who was babysitting my three-year-old at the time, noticed. She doubled what she was making for dinner and sent it home with Priscilla. I literally wept in my kitchen heating up chicken potpie that night. Someone saw me. She didn't fix the problem, but her acknowledging that there was one was really all I needed. No one died, but a dream did, and her gesture let me know it was worth grieving. She let me know I was not alone.

Imagine what a church could do with a database that says, "This person stress bakes" and "This person stress eats all the pies." Imagine a church that knew that person A buys yarn when they are stressed and person B loves to crochet but doesn't always have the material to make baby blankets.

I think this is exactly what Paul was talking about when he said we are all different parts of the body and we all have a place. The one body of Christ is made up of many parts (1 Cor 12:12–27).

When we get to the emergency phase, we don't have the bandwidth to figure out what we really need, and we don't know what to offer or what might be most helpful. In order to better be with one another in times of crisis, it is best if we already know our strengths and also what comforts us. It is not something a lot of people think about, but it comes in handy when we really need it.

I want to end this chapter by brainstorming the things that we are best at giving and also the things that give us the most comfort. We need different things. We are different people, and we just aren't all going to need the same thing. We need to be better at *asking* and also at *suggesting* and *hearing* specifically.

When someone rejects your help, it isn't personal; it is just that is not what they need right now, and if they are in a crisis, they do not have the mental space to accept what they don't really need. It is sort of the emotional equivalent of giving sparkly eight-inch heels to a food bank. It makes you feel like you did something, and then someone has to deal with what you just gave them. I have found that most people are much better at giving than they are at receiving, so we can start there.

What ways of caring for the people you love do you gravitate toward when they are hurting?

I am a feeder. When Rachel Held Evans, an author I respected deeply, died, I brought one of her good friends who lived in my town a lasagna. I have been known to drop off dinner to new moms without asking. I once made three freezer meals for someone at my church who had kiddos and was going to graduate school in a week. My first instinct is apparently to feed people.

Sometimes the most needed thing for someone in a crisis is money. Can you cover it? Costs add up in a crisis: hospital parking, takeout, gas to get back and forth, counseling or medical testing. Money is a thing we need, and I think our world would be better off if we could just be honest about that. In the midst of the COVID-19 pandemic, my family discovered we had bedbugs. How a family gets bedbugs when they haven't left the house in six weeks is beyond me. We must just be super special. I was blessed to have two friends who immediately said, "We are covering the exterminator." I still had to figure out how to keep everyone and the dog out of the house all day, how to wash every article of clothing, and how to run the vacuum nonstop, but I knew how I was going to pay for the exterminator. It may be that this isn't a way you can help out regularly, but if you have the means, you might consider adding a community emergency fund to your budget.

Some people are really good company. I am very good at sitting next to people quietly. I am very good at talking to people about their feelings. I am terrible at distracting people from their problems, but some of my friends are great at it! Know what kind of company you are. Are you doting? Are you funny? Are you good at being quiet or reading out loud to someone? My mom still talks kindly about the woman who came to my sister's bedside when my sister was a toddler in the hospital and read her a story every day. My uncle is very good at keeping everyone laughing, even at funerals. My friend Megan will let me rant on and on about how unfair someone is being. At the end of the rant, she will look at me straight-faced and say, "Let's go egg their house." This ridiculous response always makes me feel better. My friend Danielle has offered to fight more people on my behalf than I can count. I never want her to, but I am always glad she offers.

Sometimes we just need people to tell us what to do. I will always need a logistics queen when I am struggling. Even on a good day, I am terrible at remembering to put everything on the calendar and knowing when to call the doctor and not losing important paperwork. If you have the gift of organization, people need it! Help your friends who have spent all their time and energy consumed with worry. Put their important papers in a labeled folder, put their appointments in their calendar, put their pills in the pill keeper, put their shoes back in the closet.

Finally, do the stuff that just needs to be done. I don't know that anyone is "called" or "gifted" at changing diapers, driving kids around, doing dishes, or walking dogs; these are all things you do not need to be particularly skilled at to be able to do. They just need to be done. The tasks of daily life are hard on a normal week; in an impossible time, taking care of these things will lift a huge burden off of your friend in crisis.

Here is the part we are not good at thinking about. When you are in crisis, what do you need?

- Someone sitting with you? Or would you rather be left alone?
- Someone cooking for you? Ordering takeout?
- Someone doing the dishes / the laundry / the groceries?

Are you someone who does all the important stuff and then crashes or the kind of person who panics and then settles down? When in the crisis do you most need help? I think for some of us, we can get through the first few days, but at day three, we just get so worn down. Others need help up front and then find a groove. Are you prepared to go the long haul with people who have big hurts and chronic illnesses? What if they don't get better? What if they are still sad three months after their husband dies or on the first anniversary of the death?

How do you best experience comfort? I love presents. They always, 100 percent of the time, delight me and make me feel better. Some people love to be cozy and crave physical comfort; others want to spend a lot of time talking. There are no wrong answers. Do you know what you need? Sometimes we don't, and sometimes those things change. Being able to admit your own need is as important to community as being able to offer help to others. Everyone takes their turn. Spend some time figuring out your gifts and your needs. Be brave enough to share them with your community. Communal lament takes practice, and having a guide can make things a lot easier.

Prayer

As you begin to explore what ways you are great at giving care and what ways you desire to be cared for, I pray that those needs will be met. I pray that you will come to your community, and your community will care for you in a way that shows the love of Jesus to all who witness it.

5

WE CAN ADMIT WE'RE WRONG

Lament So We Change for the Better

L ament is an invitation to admit when you are wrong. A month before I went to seminary, I was afraid. I was at the Wild Goose Festival, a three-day Christian festival where everyone camps in the woods and bathes in the river. Yep, you read that correctly. My friend and I were talking about why I was so nervous about going back to school. I mean, I was going. I had quit my job, put the deposit down, cried in the dean's office until they gave me more scholarship money. But still, I wondered, what was this going to mean? What if this shaped me to be someone totally different? What if I changed? I told all of this to my deeply wise friend, and she looked at me and said, "Darlin', why would you want to commit yourself to something for three years that didn't change you?" I can't begin to describe the peace that came over me. Of course seminary would change me, just like teaching and marriage and motherhood and blogging had all changed me; this was just the next thing. Change can feel scary, but change is a gift from the Holy Spirit, its active participation in your life. Change means growing out of things that no longer fit you and growing into bigger and better ways of being: "When I was a child, I talked like a child, I thought like a child," but then "I put the ways of childhood behind me" (1 Cor 13:11).

The fact is that as we grow and change, and as we are sensitive to the Holy Spirit, we will change our minds about things. We will hopefully grow into more loving ways of living. When we grow into these more loving ways of living, we will discover that our past behaviors and beliefs may have harmed people. Our past (and current) ways of being may be wrong. That's where lament comes in. Lament is not only a vital way of speaking to God but an opportunity to turn away from things that we did or believed that were wrong and embrace a more loving way of being in the world.

Belovedness over Rightness

In order to admit we are wrong, we have to admit that our belovedness does not rest on the correctness of our opinions. God won't cancel us. We can be wrong about every single thing and still God would proclaim that we are beloved. This is true for you. Please, let that sink in. But if this is true for you (and it totally is), then it is also true for the person you can't wait for God to judge and for the person who just gets on your last nerve. *You* don't have to be around them all the time, but it is important to remember that God is sort of obsessed with them, wants to be with them all the time, and is just *wild* about loving them. It may seem hard to grasp, but that doesn't mean it is not true.

When I think about what all this changing our minds and lamenting looks like, I think of my friend who was basically raised in a cult. She likes to say that she was wrong about the age of the earth, and about money, and about sexual morality, and about whether Jesus rode a dinosaur, so she is at least willing to consider she might be wrong about a stance she currently holds. She is just a completely amazing listener. She is so curious about the world and how to get better information. She almost delights in being wrong: "Oh! Look! Better information. I was wrong before, but I don't have to be like that anymore! I am making strides!"

We cannot base our belovedness on whether we are right. One of my friends from a more conservative church once said that it felt like she was raised on the trinity of the Father, Son, and Holy Scriptures. As long as you had the right beliefs regarding the Bible, then you were the right kind of Christian who was right with God, and that put you in the theological club labeled "loved by God." I have been to these kinds of churches, where being wrong about anything is really terrifying. There is no room for lament when you aren't allowed to be wrong.

Lest you think being a progressive protects from this thinking, I assure you, it goes both ways. Sometimes, I think that the liberal church is in danger of worshiping the idol of right thinking. If we have all the right answers for all the theoretical questions and are still assholes (or worse yet, are assholes because of it), then what the heck are we doing? We are supposed to be a people of *grace*. We are proclaiming that Jesus is for everyone, that God includes everyone, that the table is open, and we are all siblings in Christ. Yet we do not give anyone the space to disagree or change their mind. We are so hell-bent on being *right* because we are still terrified that we might be wrong. Neither our right thinking nor our good theology are what makes us beloved. Embracing that understanding leaves enough room for us to reverse course. God loves us no matter what, but we need to change our minds when we are wrong.

We are so bad at admitting we are wrong because the world tells us we are somehow less-than if we don't have it all together. Being wrong is scary, and we live in a world that condemns people for their past mistakes. But *praise God*! Our salvation and our worth are not based on our rightness. They are not based on whether we have the correct ideology. Our worth is based on a God who makes us, from dust, in God's own image and *then* calls us "very good." If we really believed this at our core—that regardless of what we believe or how we act, we are the essence of "very good"— we would feel safer admitting that sometimes what we once believed, deep down, was wrong. But instead, Christianity tends to be marked by a tribalism in which you must think exactly as I think or you will be banished from the inside group. That's rightness over belovedness, and that's not lament. Lament invites us into trusting that God loves us. It frees us from basing our worth on how correct we are. A people who are so full of God's love that they are unafraid to admit when they were wrong, lament the hurt they caused, and seek to repair the damage they have done is a people that could change the world.

This kind of lament, the kind that invites us into a space that says "I was wrong and I want to do better" is the antithesis of the Christianity so many of us were taught. It is scary the first time you decide you are going to publicly confess, but it gets easier. It helps if you have watched people go before you. In the traditional Communion liturgy, right at the beginning,

right before we pass the peace, we confess to God that we have fallen short:
We have not loved as we should have. There were things that should be done
that were left undone. There were things that were left undone that should
have been done. I love this part of the liturgy. I need to be reminded that
I am not the only one who fails. I need to pass the peace to those who have
also been wrong. We need to interact with one another as we are: fully loved
and forgiven people who are not always right about everything, who cause
real damage and break real relationships and are perfectly loved by God.

I know it took me believing that I was fully loved before I *realized* that
I was fully loved, even if I was wrong. The religion I was raised with was
very clear on the *very big God* thing but not so clear on the *very big grace*
thing. I spent a lot of my time worried that even the smallest decision could
be wrong, and God cared about *everything* because *God was a very big
God*. God is a very big God, but this very big God doesn't need us to get
everything right the first time, or even ever, in order to have us do God's
good work in the world. Instead, God invites us to start where we are and let
God continue to change us. Lament marks our change, shows that God is
working in us, that the Holy Spirit still does good work in us and the world.

Changing Your Mind Out Loud

Wrong theology has consequences. I know this because my own theology
caused a lot of hurt before I was able to change my position and publicly
lament. I was raised to believe that God loves all people but that same-sex
relationships were not "God's best." I am grieved by the hurt I caused and
sad for the relationships that suffered because of my heartfelt (but wrong)
beliefs. I am grateful for the grace that allowed me to continue to be in
relationship with the people I hurt even as I've continued to learn and
grow. We all need to be better at saying we are wrong, and our confessions
need to be public.

It was the suicide rate that stopped my theology dead in its tracks. While
only 4.6 percent of the total US population attempts suicide, 30–40 percent
of LGBTQ people do. I wasn't sure what I thought about homosexuality,
but I knew that this statistic grieved God. I heard these numbers on my
way to school. My carmate, now my best friend, is the faculty advisor of the

Gay-Straight Alliance and the only out faculty member at the high school where we worked. I was shocked and saddened, and I wondered what could change that statistic. I wanted to know what could be done.

As someone who had spent most of her life in a conservative Christian culture, there was a lot I didn't know. And there were a lot of things I "knew" that turned out to be wrong. I had heard, in church even, that homosexuality always arose out of a place of brokenness, from abuse or estrangement from a parent. I heard that homosexual partnerships were dysfunctional and almost never monogamous. I heard that gay marriages didn't count and certainly weren't honored by God.

But then, through a very long commute and an honest friendship, I was exposed to a marriage I respected deeply firsthand that contradicted all the things I thought I knew. These two women were (and still are) happy and healthy and whole. Where was the obvious dysfunction? Where was the lack of sacredness? I couldn't find it. I sometimes envied their relationship. Then a friend from college—I had been so sad at his coming out—got married and was so obviously better off for it. My husband and I had prayed long and hard about whether to even attend the reception, and I am so grateful that we went. Our friend's new husband was everything we had hoped for in a partner for him—supportive, kind, and totally in love with our friend. It was impossible to care that our friend didn't marry a woman.

In my Southern Baptist church, where there were no gay people (not openly, anyway), I had heard that homosexual relationships were not God's best. But in my actual life, I witnessed happy and fulfilled gay friends whose marriages were enviable. These relationships didn't look second-rate compared to mine. They looked awesome.

I decided I didn't know what I thought. For at least a year, if someone would have asked me about my stance on homosexuality, I would have said, "I don't know. It seems like it would be really hard to navigate, and I am not experiencing it, so I don't know." I had always heard that gay-affirming Christians were just bending to cultural pressure. Ironically, I was desperately afraid of the church culture that told me that if I switched sides, as it were, I would become a "them"—"that kind of Christian." Maybe "that kind of Christian" still loved Jesus, but they were kind of a sellout. I didn't want to be a them. I didn't want to be a sellout. I didn't want to lose my pack.

I also worried about what the "thems" would think of me. Was it too late? How do you tell the person that has already become your best friend that you once did not affirm her relationship but now you do? How do you explain to the best man at your wedding that even being invited to his wedding caused a bit of a crisis of faith? What if you are too late? What if you switch from an us to a them but they don't want you? What if you aren't an us or a them and you are left with no pack?

Through all the wrestling, the praying, the crying, the searching, the praying, the reading, reading, reading, I could not get the suicide statistic out of my head. I did find strong theological thinking for a gay-affirming Christian stance, but that is not what moved my heart. Forty percent! Forty percent of my LGBTQ friends and students would attempt suicide or already had. I knew in my heart that this desperately grieved God.

My LGBTQ friends told me that my theology was part of the problem. While I didn't endorse the hate speech of Westboro Baptist Church, I was essentially telling people (but only if they asked outright) that there was something less-than in the way they were built.

I could not tell you exactly where, or how, but my switch in theology, my belief that God affirms gay relationships, was mostly a work of the Holy Spirit. However, changing my personal beliefs was not enough. I needed to publicly lament my poor theology.

Changing your mind publicly and lamenting out loud, to others, that your actions or beliefs (or both) have hurt people is terrifying. Sometimes, when we faithfully follow Jesus, really scary things happen. The Holy Spirit gently and patiently nudged me away from a theology that said only heterosexual marriages were acceptable and toward one that affirmed all sexual orientations as beautifully created by God. And while it happened in inches for me, I went public with my change in belief just after the 2016 Orlando nightclub shooting. The public reality of the consequences of my old theology pushed me to do so. I knew that part of my work of lament was to explain how I had moved from one position to the other.

Lamenting publicly, saying I was wrong (and to be clear, I was wrong), was maybe going to cost me some of those relationships I treasured. But it was what needed to happen. Public lament is a step in the repentance God calls us to, and the cost of losing my relationships was pennies compared to the things my queer friends had lost when they came out. If we were wrong in public and it hurt people, it is imperative that we repent. I was late to the party, but I was received in love. This is what I learned from my LGBTQ friends: God honors repentance. If God is asking you to change your mind, if the Holy Spirit is moving your heart, God will not abandon you.

God honors repentance, and the people who have been pushed out of the church, rejected because of who they are and what they think, are not interested in doing that to other people. The journey from one theology to another can be scary, and it often doesn't follow our preferred timing, or even a straight line. But if you feel something stirring, I pray that you honor that stir. It is OK to change your mind. Just as God embraces your emotions of lament, he embraces your ability to grow and change as you learn and lament.

When I lamented by saying publicly that I had learned I was wrong and changed my mind, I did not have that many followers on social media. I had never taken a public stance. I could have just let everyone assume I had always been affirming, but I didn't think that was fair. Out loud, public lament has the potential to free not just yourself but also others who need to confess as well. Very often, we believe we are the only person in our community who thinks a certain way or has harmed people in a certain way. That is almost always not true. Public lament can lead to others joining in the walk toward freedom.

This public lament also meant aligning myself with what I had previously seen as "the other side," which meant having views that oppose those of some of the people I love. One of the things that has happened as my politics have moved more and more to the left is that my parents and I aren't exactly on the same page. It's a hard thing, but not a bad one, and it gives me a great way to talk to my kids about (1) how it is OK to change your mind and (2) not everyone will agree on everything. When we talk about politics, about what we believe, it is good for me to tell them that I used to believe something else, that people whom we love and respect *do* believe something else, that we make the best decisions with the information we have and then we make better choices, that it is always OK to hear other people out and see when we are wrong. It has been powerful to model to my daughters how we can correct course humbly instead of digging our heels in about something.

I used to believe that having all the right answers was a way that I could best defend my faith against the world. Lament was seen as a weakness rather than a regular part of realigning myself with the Holy Spirit. It has been freeing to realize we don't have to defend God. We don't have to protect God's thinking and theology and explain to everyone just how exactly God is working it out so that we can still worship a good God. Our theology doesn't have to be perfect. We are allowed to not know things. We can have questions like "What about this?" and answers like "I am still working that out." God doesn't need us to be right all the time. We can rearrange our ideas when we have more and better information. When we lament publicly, this allows everyone the freedom to do the same.

Lamenting Our Collective Past

There are people who got it wrong in history. Christopher Columbus didn't find a new way to get to India, and he didn't "discover" any land that didn't already belong to people. Andrew Jackson killed and terrorized indigenous people with the Indian Removal Act. George Washington owned slaves.

The church historically doesn't fare much better. Crusades in the name of Jesus killed millions. Women were burned at the stake for being heretics and witches against the holy order of things. Slavery was defended as preordained and part of the way God hoped to work in the world. People have been wrong in the name of Jesus since the resurrection. The Methodists, the Baptists, the Lutherans (really everyone but the Quakers or the Mennonites) were wrong about what the Bible said about slavery. Denominations split over whether pastors could own slaves. Christian denominations in the United States have contributed to discouraging women in the workplace and equal wages for equal work, citing family values as a reason the patriarchy should be placed on a pedestal. Church sex abuse is so rampant it necessitated its own hashtag, #ChurchToo.

Though Christians have clearly been incredibly wrong about many things, Christians are usually terrible at admitting it. Churches, denominations, and individual members don't typically say, "Hey, we used to believe this thing, and now we think we might be wrong, so we're going to figure out what's right and do better." Instead, they quietly move toward a more neutral position, avoid talking about a position that might be controversial, or simply switch positions quietly and act like they have always been that way.

When a church changes policies, they often scrub their websites and histories of ever having the bad policies in the first place. If you talk to most Methodists, they love to tell you about how they have always been social-justice oriented. Most will leave out the part about how the AME (American Methodist Episcopal) denomination was created because the Methodists wouldn't let Black people make decisions for their *own churches*. In fact, the United Methodist Church made the AME pay for their first church twice over when the AME church decided to split off rather than be run by a white pastor.

I don't like that my religion is synonymous with the oppressor to many, but I can't (and shouldn't) deny that truth. Christians need to be honest about the ways we got it wrong. We're all human and we are all going to be wrong about things, but we cannot just sweep those things under the rug. We must be able to lament the ways that we were wrong so that we can work toward a different way.

Christians are extremely good at avoiding stating a clear position and instead using complicated insider "God talk" to avoid discussing anything they don't want to. If you want to figure out what a church thinks, you will probably have to do some investigating of your own. I love using the Church Clarity website as a resource for understanding what churches really stand for. Church Clarity reads church newsletters and websites and rates a church on whether it is clear about its views on homosexuality and women in leadership. This organization's work is vital because so many churches don't want to be called out. They don't want to be wrong. They won't let women in the pulpit and won't support gay marriage, but they sure won't tell anyone that.

It should matter to us a lot whether our truth is clear. We are a people who say that Jesus is the way, the truth, and the light. But as Christians, our identity shouldn't come from our rightness on particular issues. Our identity should come from the solid belief that we are beloved by God, that we are children of God and co-heirs with Christ. When identity comes from belovedness over rightness, Christians should be the best at changing our minds, admitting we are wrong, and seeking to repair the damage we did in the past. God loves us thoroughly before and after we change our minds. Resting in that can allow us to freely explore when there might be a better way.

No One Has It All Figured Out

Our society completely scoffs at the idea of admitting fault. Our politicians defend votes from thirty years ago that they know are wrong. Having the courage to say, "You know what? I heard better information, and now I don't think that way anymore" somehow, in the eyes of our culture, makes you someone who can't be trusted. Personally, I'm impressed with a person who can be corrected graciously. I would rather have a leader who always uses the best information they have rather than one who insists they are right regardless of the new information presented. We are a church that claims God is always moving, that God's mercies are new every morning, and that God makes all things new. Sometimes, that means shifting positions on some things—being wrong and realizing that might be really good news.

The day that my husband and I told our Bible study who had met in our house for six years or so that they would not be meeting in our home next semester because we had too many theological differences with the church was also the day the group studied Acts 10 and 11. The day that we studied Peter, Peter who thought one thing about the gentiles, and then the Holy Spirit showed up and tore in half what Peter once thought was sacred.

Sometimes we are wrong, even in our purest intentions of what we believe God wants. We need to hold such things loosely. It is hard to suss out what is holiness and what is cultural. What if it was OK to change our minds? Lament is the piece that allows us to do so within our community and in a way that does not rewrite history. We live in a day and age where anyone who disagrees with us is evil, is lying, is wrong. If we cast the other as "those horrible things," then it is hard for us to see ourselves as wrong because then we would be other, be lying, be wrong in some kind of existential way that could not be changed.

I was lucky when I moved from not gay-affirming to completely gay-affirming. I wasn't a big deal. I didn't have any books to take off the shelves at conservative stores because of it. I wasn't going against a denomination that controlled my health care, my paycheck, my housing. I did not have a lot to lose. I have known so many people who changed their ideologies and lost so much. Still, they will tell you it is the right thing. Christians should celebrate moving on theological positions. Sarah Bessey likes to say that if you remain the same in your faith through ten, twenty, forty years, then you are probably not paying attention. I have found this to be true.

We don't have everything figured out. We won't have everything figured out this side of heaven. Church history is full of terrible horrible things done in the name of Jesus. Every major church denomination has benefitted from the financial legacy of slavery; I don't care if your church is in the North or the South: you've benefitted. Churches have and continue to exist on the free labor of women they won't employ. We have not always gotten it right, we do not always get it right, we will continue to blow it big-time as we seek to do the work of the Lord. People have a right not to trust the church; we don't always act in the best interest of the people.

At eight years old, I gave myself faithfully to the work of the gospel, and ever since, the work of the gospel has been expanding in rings moving outward like a rock making ripples in a pond. Every time I think that God has called someone out of bounds, the Holy Spirit has a way of quietly winking at me and saying, "You so sure about that, Pastor Abby?" God excels at making me uncomfortable. God's grace is always willing to move past my understanding.

That's exactly what God did with Peter, and it's exactly what he does with us today. It begins with someone who is clearly *for God* and so, so sure that some people are in and some people are out. Then God always, always takes the side of the ones who are out. The side of the poor, those with less power, less privilege, less money, less of a right to be there. This freaks people out, and you know what? It freaks me out too. It never ceases to freak me out. But I know deep in my soul that siding with those who are the least in these things is good news for everyone.

Changing Your Mind Is Holy: The Bible Tells Me So

It is very good news that our goodness does not depend on us being right all the time. God's grace is *so much bigger* than that. There is no opinion I could have that is so wrong that it will separate me from the love of God. Will it make God sad? Yes. Will it grieve the Holy Spirit? Yes, it will. God cares very deeply about what we believe and how we treat our brothers and sisters in Christ. I think, just as God showed up to Peter in a dream at the house of a gentile, God shows up to us in a myriad of ways, allowing us to see the ways in which the old has gone and the new has come and how much God wants us to welcome everyone. But if we are going to be ready for the new way, we must lament the old.

Peter's 180-degree turn in Acts is one of the most powerful mind-changing events in the history of the church. Acts 10 tells the story, first by telling us about Cornelius:

> There was a man in Caesarea by the name of Cornelius, a centurion in what was called the Italian Regiment. He was a deeply religious man who reverenced God, as did all his household. He made many charitable gifts to the people and was a real man of prayer. About three o'clock one afternoon he saw perfectly clearly in a dream an angel of God coming into his room, approaching him, and saying, "Cornelius!"
>
> He stared at the angel in terror, and said, "What is it, Lord?"
>
> The angel replied, "Your prayers and your deeds of charity have gone up to Heaven and are remembered before God. Now send men to Joppa for a man called Simon, who is also known as Peter. He is staying as a guest with another Simon, a tanner, whose house is down by the sea."
>
> When the angel who had spoken to him had gone, Cornelius called out for two of his house-servants and a devout soldier, who was one of his personal attendants. He told them the whole story and then sent them off to Joppa. (Acts 10:1–8 PHILLIPS)

And then we hear Peter's side of the story:

Peter went up about mid-day on to the flat roof of the house to pray. He became very hungry and longed for something to eat. But while the meal was being prepared he fell into a trance and saw the heavens open and something like a great sheet descending upon the earth, let down by its four corners. In it were all kinds of animals, reptiles and birds. Then came a voice which said to him, "Get up, Peter, kill and eat!"

But Peter said, "Never, Lord! For not once in my life have I ever eaten anything common or unclean."

Then the voice spoke to him a second time, "You must not call what God has cleansed common." (Acts 10:9–15 PHILLIPS)

After all this, Peter and Cornelius come together. Peter connects the dots and realizes that he was wrong. That God was doing a new thing, and that he, Peter, was to announce it instead of condemn it. Peter then proclaims,

"In solemn truth I can see now that God is no respecter of persons, but that in every nation the man who reverences him and does what is right is acceptable to him! He has sent his message to the sons of Israel by giving us the good news of peace through Jesus Christ—he is the Lord of us all. You must know the story of Jesus of Nazareth—why, it has spread through the whole of Judea, beginning with Galilee after the baptism that John proclaimed. You must have heard how God anointed him with the power of the Holy Spirit, of how he went about doing good and healing all who suffered from the devil's power—because God was with him. Now we are eye-witnesses of everything that he did, both in the Judean country and in Jerusalem itself, and yet they murdered him by hanging him on a cross. But on the third day God raised that same Jesus and let him be clearly seen, not indeed by the whole people, but by witnesses whom God had previously chosen. We are those witnesses, we who ate and drank with him after he had risen from the dead! Moreover, we are the men whom he commanded to preach to the people and bear fearless witness to the fact that he is the one appointed by God to be the judge of both the living and the dead.

It is to him that all the prophets bear witness, that every man who believes in him may receive forgiveness of sins through his name." While Peter was still speaking these words the Holy Spirit fell upon all who were listening to his message. The Jewish believers who had come with Peter were absolutely amazed that the gift of the Holy Spirit was being poured out on Gentiles also; for they heard them speaking in foreign tongues and glorifying God.

Then Peter exclaimed, "Could anyone refuse water or object to these men being baptised—men who have received the Holy Spirit just as we did ourselves?"

And he gave orders for them to be baptised in the name of Jesus Christ. Afterwards they asked him to stay with them for some days. (Acts 10:34–48 PHILLIPS)

I wonder what the Jews who were with Peter thought of this reversal of position. I wonder if they are a little afraid: "Wait a minute . . . we have put all our eggs in this basket, this brand-new religion, and already Peter is changing the rules? What does this mean for Peter's judgment? What does this mean for the special place for the Israelites?" I mean, these people are already being hounded at home for stepping away from their religion, and now Peter is just going to let all the gentiles in too? What would their mothers think?!

But there Peter is, instantly professing that he had thought one thing and, in the blink of an eye, God had reversed his decision. God is saying yes to the gentiles. Later, in Galatians, Peter argues again for full gentile inclusion, saying that circumcision is a burden that God finds unnecessary to be a Christian (Gal 6:15). Peter has again changed his mind. Did God change God's mind? I would say no, but not all theologians would agree. I think that God reveals God's self differently in different times and to different generations. I also think God is always pushing us to widen the circle and set more places at the table, to ask ourselves, "Who isn't here?" To search them out and then to listen to why they don't feel welcome in our churches and perhaps change our policies in the name of a bigger love. I think a church that admits it was wrong for all the right reasons would be a beautiful gift to the world.

Practice Makes (Im)Perfect

I love to watch people change their minds. People who are humble enough to hear other people and know that they don't know everything, to say, "Oh, OK, I see that I hurt you." I know that our absolute knee-jerk reaction is to defend ourselves: "I am *not* wrong, I did *not* hurt you, I *am* good." People criticizing your behavior doesn't mean that *you* are bad, though very, very many of us are afraid that's exactly what criticism means. Having some wrong thinking or some unhealthy theology is not the same thing as being a wrong and terrible human being. You can still be beloved by God and also totally wrong. Learning to hear criticism and different opinions without thinking they are an affront to your belovedness is a great first step to being able to lament when you are wrong.

It can feel really horrible the first time you admit that you were wrong and ask for forgiveness, but I promise it gets easier. As a classroom teacher, I promised my students that if I did something wrong in front of the class, I would also apologize in front of the class. The first rule of my classroom was "Be Kind"—I had a giant sign hanging in front of the room. I was not always kind. I was often the cheekiest person in a room full of teenagers. Learning to apologize in front of them softened my heart to them and also theirs to me. It allowed us to see each other as people, not just as a student or a teacher. It also allowed us more space to explore because we knew if we did something wrong, we could apologize. Lamenting when we are wrong is more than just apologizing. That is a good start, but God asks for more.

It's important to take steps to make things right. As Daniel Tiger tells us, "Saying sorry is the first step. Then, how can I help?" If you have hurt someone, it is important to not just say sorry but see if you can make it right. It is also important to lament your complicit nature with wrongdoing and then stop doing that thing. As I tell my daughters, if you are sorry, you will stop. Are you a white person hanging a "Black Lives Matter" flag in your neighborhood and also profiting off the displacement of your Black neighbors? That is not lament. That isn't even allyship. That is making yourself feel better. Are you unwilling to actually feel the consequences of your lament? I know this sounds harsh, and it is scary. Walking with God often means giving up comfort, but it also means finding deeper resonance with the kingdom of God.

There are endless ways to rethink lament. When you submit the idea of being right all the time to God, that is really fertile ground for God to grow beautiful things in.

Prayer

It is not lost on me that continually I am asking you to do hard things. This may be the hardest thing of all. Being wrong can be such a gift to us if only we embrace it. I pray that you will be so grounded in your belovedness that you will be open to the Holy Spirit changing your mind. I pray that you will be open to a bigger God, a bigger grace, a bigger community. May you experience your belovedness together.

6

WE CAN HEAR THOSE IN NEED

Lament So We Can Be with People Who Hurt

Lamenting that the world is not right and that our neighbors are hurting is one of the ways we can better connect with one another. In a world where everything comes at us all the time, where we have more information about more crises in more places than ever before, it is sometimes hard to even take in the things we are hearing. Scientists long ago figured out that we are not designed to think about worldwide problems like global warming or massive amounts of death. We literally cannot comprehend them. I think this is the reason that, very often, a single story grips us so effectively. It is impossible to wrap our minds around thousands of people dying in a natural disaster. It is much easier to be sad for a family who has lost their child in a freak accident at Disney World. We often grab on to a single story where we can know a name and face because humans are designed to display compassion and empathy in relationship.

Statistically, most of us are only in relationship with people who are just like us. Most of us have few friends who have had experiences that are very different from our own. It turns out that it is a lot easier to have friends who see the world as we see it and who have experiences with the world that match our own. Everything feels safer and less confusing when the world works the same for everyone we know. But the world does not work for everyone in the same ways. People with more power, more money, and more privilege have an easier time than those who don't. My husband is sometimes surprised by the ways that men at the church attempt to talk to him about issues I should be in charge of. It surprises him, but it doesn't surprise me. I have been a woman my whole life. I know how some people talk to women. I know who underestimates me.

Sometimes the best way for us to understand our neighbors' pain is to lament with them. In order to understand what our neighbors are going through, we need to be able to hear them. We need to be able to sit with their lament. Then we need to be able to lament with our neighbor, because we are hurting when our neighbors are hurting, whether we know it or not. We are all connected. By understanding our neighbors (especially the ones who are not like us) and their unique experiences of suffering, we can join in their lament and ask God for a better world for everyone.

When I started preaching at New Hope United Methodist Church, I also started going to the Bible study that many of the church's neighbors regularly attended. They were not like me. We lived in completely different realities. I have lived in the same house for ten years, and it's a house that my family owns. My family has had lean financial years, sure, but we always made ends meet. Our lives don't contain a lot of chaos. I could have given you a list of social problems, but all of them were merely theoretical to me. They weren't social problems that were hurting me or the people I loved. This was not the case for those who went to Bible study at New Hope. Many were homeless, and those who lived in homes rented. These neighbors lived paycheck to paycheck and relied on government services to eat and manage chronic health conditions. I guess I'd known about aggressive gentrification and shady real estate practices, but it came crashing into my reality one day when code enforcement was unleashed on the neighborhood behind the church.

If you're not familiar, calling code enforcement is a shady practice realtors often engage when they are attempting to flip whole neighborhoods of houses at a time. They call code enforcement every day until the city makes the rounds and issues citations for code violations. Then the people who live in the impoverished neighborhood have to spend all their time and energy fixing whatever thing they have been living with for fifteen years. The items that they're forced to spend resources fixing are unsightly but usually don't actually present a danger to anyone. Maybe there are some steps that are safe but not properly painted; maybe there is a safely parked trailer that happens to have a flat tire. Whatever the case may be, if the people are renters, then the owner of the house gets hit with the fine. Sometimes the owner of the house gets hit with multiple fines. This is a giant pain in their butt, but don't worry! The next day, the realtor offers to buy the house, kicks the people who have been renting out overnight, and jacks the price up so it is no longer affordable. The people who have lived in the house for fifteen years are out with nowhere to go. The code enforcement people strike fear into the hearts of my neighbors in a way I didn't understand until I started eating and praying with them every week. Before that, I kind of thought of the code enforcement people as perhaps a bit annoying but pretty innocuous. I liked lawns getting mowed and the trash not being allowed out front. I didn't understand the darker side of this public service until I prayed with the people it was hurting. All of a sudden, I wanted to consider both sides of the policies, because I saw how much people were hurting. I wanted to lament with the people because I heard their problems.

Being in the Chaos of Life

A few years ago, I resigned from my job when my husband still hadn't quite found one, and I literally had no idea where we would live in six months. I was having a particularly hard time. Everything felt up in the air, and the uncertainty was wearing me down. During this period, I left voice messages back and forth with a friend who had experienced a similar state of uncertainty the year before: waiting, not knowing, wanting, and being afraid of wanting. She was in that place of transition the year before me, waiting for her husband to be offered a job so she knew where she was moving, seemingly stuck midleap with no place to land. She has been in this place that I found myself in. She knew how worthless the platitudes were. Instead, she gave it to me straight. She told me that my greatest wishes could be granted and that she was certainly praying for that. She told me that my greatest fears could be realized and that she was certainly praying against that. She told me that no matter what, on the other end of this, I would be there, she would be there, and God would be there. With us.

When people experience huge problems, like when they don't have safe housing or their kids don't have access to healthy food or high-quality education, we want big answers and grand gestures. When I was in total chaos, I thought that I needed answers and completion and for the waiting to end. But what I really needed was for the people around me, and for God, to show up and be with me.

My sister and I both live in Atlanta. She attended the births of both of my children, and I've been there for all four of hers. We have learned how each other labors. I am so grateful that she was there with me and also that I got to be there with her. It seems the thing that helped the most with the pain of childbirth for both of us was having someone there to mark time. To count through the contractions, to say, "I saw you do that, that one looked like it hurt. OK, I saw you do that so I know you can do this next one. OK! We are halfway done. Only three more counts left." We don't feel each other's pain. But we do stand with each other. We do not look away.

On Being *With*

When I started teaching in the inner city, I had all these ideas about how a high school worked, and what the policies are for, and why they're good. Once I started teaching, though, I got to know the kids. I got to know how hard they were trying and how impossibly difficult their lives were. And it broke me. I came home almost every day with essays in my hands about how hard these kids had it. But being with them had to mean that I was with them, not above them with legalistic policies, and not swooping in for them without any understanding of what they experienced and what they needed.

Perhaps it is my ten years of English teaching, but I find *with* to be such a profound preposition. Prepositions, by definition, describe the relationship between two things. I used to tell my students that a preposition went anywhere a mouse could go. The way we use prepositions can tell us a lot about how we think of our neighbors. For example, when we think about relationships we have with people who are different from us, do we think about advocating *for* people or acting *above* them in decision-making? As *below* them or just *around* them? Or are we *with* them, really with our neighbors in their suffering. So many times, we think what someone needs is something from us or for us to fix something when what they really need is for someone to be with them.

Understanding your neighbor and offering yourself in solidarity is a lot harder than it sounds. Lamenting with people can be tricky. Believe me, I have screwed it up enough for all of us. I showed up to teach at a low-income high school where 99 percent of the students were Black. I thought I understood them and their reality. I didn't. I didn't understand what they did or why they did it. I did not understand how hard their lives were. I did not understand that poverty means a higher likelihood of trauma and that some of what I was doing in order to "relate" or "reach the kids" was actually compounding that trauma. I once asked the kids to write and share the scariest moment of their life. I thought they would tell me about a roller coaster or a time their brother played a prank on them. Instead, I was inundated with stories about traumatic episodes of violence. Then I did nothing with those stories. I just read them and checked them off for credit.

This wasn't good praxis. It wasn't good solidarity. It was not lamenting with them. Yet when I told people about these errors, the world offered me so much more solidarity for "sacrificing" and "helping" these kids than was ever offered to the children whose *teacher* was retraumatizing them! I was never accountable for retraumatizing children in the name of education. No one who taught me how to be a teacher even warned me that this was a possibility. I had a whole degree in public education, and I still did not know how to be *with* the kids first and *for* them second. In order to be in solidarity with people, it is really important to be *with* people, not *for* people. We have all been talked down to. No one, *no one* likes it! Don't be the one doing the talking down. Assume that people are the experts of their own experiences. Make like the protagonist of *The Magic School Bus*: Stay curious, and don't be afraid to get messy. Community is messy. People are messy. You will not always get solidarity right.

I have learned from pastoring in a community far different from the one I was used to that the people in it are far better at understanding what their neighborhoods need than I am. So many of my ideas fell flat, while the caretaker who had lived in the neighborhood for years had ones that served the community so much better. Did it hurt my ego? Yes. But is serving my neighborhood about my ego? It is not. We need to assume that the people who live in the community know what they need more than we do. This is how we stay in solidarity with our neighbor. We pay attention and believe that they are the experts in their own life. We do this because this is what Christ did for us. We lament in solidarity.

Confronting Privilege in Lament

Sometimes, we think that being with someone and lamenting with someone are about mutuality. You hear my problems, and I hear yours. In other words, you earn the right for me to hear your problems if you also listen to mine. But people with privilege do not have the right to ask people who are being oppressed to understand us. If we instead take our own lament to our God and our people, then we make the space to lament with those in our community who need God to advocate on their behalf because the systems aren't fair to them. When we have dealt with our own pain, it is much easier to bear witness to those who are living very different experiences than our own. When we honor our own pain, we are way less likely to shout, "But I am hurting too!" when someone tells us of their pain. We are better able to see the privileges we hold and the ones our neighbors aren't afforded because we know this isn't some kind of competition.

But societally, we often look away, ignoring the things that make us uncomfortable, pretending everything is fine because we don't know what to say. We don't grow up talking about systemic privilege, about race, about death. We don't grow up saying, "This is wrong and unfair and hurting people, and someone should do something about it." We especially don't grow up talking about the systems that we benefit from.

One of the ways to be with someone, to show solidarity and learn to lament well with your neighbor, is to learn how to talk openly about the things you were raised to ignore or whisper about. While I had experience talking about race because both my husband and I worked in predominantly Black schools, I had to learn to talk about race on another level because my daughter came home talking about it. She interrupted our cookie making during Christmas break her first year of school to let me know that the flour was white, and so were we. When I asked her what that meant she rolled her eyes and pointed at her skin and then my skin and said,

"Mom, you got this too." She was the only white child in her class, and she was wondering if I had noticed our whiteness because I hadn't talked about it. White people are generally the only people uncomfortable talking about race because, as the people most often centered in the conversation, we never have to. Black people, Asian people, Latinx people, they know how to talk about race. They have to in order to understand their own reality.

People can get past an honest gaffe. Believe me, I have shoved my foot in my mouth more times than most people. You can say, "I am here to talk about it, or not, what do you want?" I know that seems totally terrifying, but it is the right move. We need to be able to talk about it, whatever it might be—and also not talk about it if that is what they need. The way to do either of these things is with each other. We do it together. We carry one another's burdens, and we seek to be in right relationship with one another. We name each burden and we are not afraid because we are blessed when we choose to lament with our neighbor.

Love Your Neighbor, Lament with Your Neighbor

A few years ago, two divorces in a row rocked my congregation. The people involved were high-profile couples at our church. You know the kind— people who were on all the committees and doing all the right things, people outsiders would have said had perfect lives. But all of a sudden (it seemed to us on the outside, anyway), they announced they were getting divorced. We were all shocked. When I went to talk to one of the women, I learned for the first time how bad her marriage had been.

It would have been so, so, so easy to just insist it wasn't that bad. Most of her friends were insisting it wasn't that bad. But it was. It was that bad. She needed to leave, and I didn't understand until I was with her in it. I was raised in a pretty emotionally healthy family, and I married a man who is not abusive. I didn't understand what being her was like. I couldn't. I had to sit with her and trust her in her own story so I could slowly understand. People would have looked at our situations and told you that she was the one who should be lamenting, who should be checking her privilege. But in that moment, with this particular situation, this was not the case. We were mutually with each other.

I tell this story because I think that God calls us to be with people, to lament with people, to advocate with people. But if we do it *for* them and not *with* them, we can do a lot of damage. When these divorces shook our little church community, it freaked a lot of us out. It made us realize this devastating thing was closer than we knew. Most people wanted to swoop in and fix it. But we weren't living that life, and we didn't actually know the ins and the outs. We needed to be with these couples before we could advocate for them, and if we weren't, we were going to hurt them.

I do not know that there is anything more powerful than "God with us," which is what *Emmanuel* means. I need a God who decided to feel my pain and experience human joy. I need a God who has stubbed his toe and cried for her children. When I was a very young mother with two children under the age of two, I needed a God who I believed was holding me as I was rocking my little ones. I needed a God who had been there, who had been here on Earth. Knowing this God helps me be with other people, to lament with them.

Centering Others Is Holy: The Bible Tells Me So

Leviticus is the book of the Bible with all the details of the law the Hebrew people were expected to follow. There are all these boring bits about how many cubits things are supposed to be and how many times people need to wash stuff. Then, in the midst of all the boring stuff, there are all these rules about how to treat the widows, the refugees, the orphans, the people that the most powerful in society would likely have no contact with. Over and over again, Levitical law asks us to be with people who are not like us, to be hospitable to the stranger, the widow, the orphan, the refugee—to treat those who are different from us as part of our community. I can't help but think that this has as much to do with changing our own hearts as it has to do with caring for them. When we push people to the sidelines of society, we pretty easily convince ourselves we have nothing in common with those people. But it is very hard to pretend that you hold nothing in common when you live in the same neighborhood, get your groceries from the same place, or when your kids go to the same elementary school.

Yes, the Israelites were supposed to live differently, to set themselves apart, but not so they could isolate themselves. Instead, it was so that people could be invited into the ways of God. Leviticus asks the judges to model a just rending because God is just: "You shall not render an unjust judgment; you shall not be partial to the poor or defer to the great: with justice you shall judge your neighbor" (19:15 NRSV). Levitical law was serious about how to treat immigrants: "The foreigner residing among you must be treated as your native-born. Love them as yourself, for you were foreigners in Egypt. I am the Lord your God" (Lev 19:34). The Israelites were asked to live differently, to set their society up differently so that they would be interdependent, so that they would need each other, so that they could lament with those who needed the most change. Leviticus also specifically asks God's people to be inefficient in their farming practices in order to remember the poor: "When you reap the harvest of your land, you shall not reap to the very edges of your field, or gather the gleanings of your harvest. You shall not strip your vineyard bare, or gather the fallen grapes of your vineyard; you shall leave them for the poor and the alien: I am the Lord your God" (19:9–10 NRSV).

This system of interdependence is how Ruth, a refugee, becomes a part of Jesus's ancestral line. Ruth isn't an Israelite, but she marries one. Then disaster strikes: Ruth's husband dies, and Ruth's brother-in-law dies. This leaves her mother-in-law, Naomi, with no good options either. The easiest thing for Ruth to do would be to cut her losses. She could go back to her people and say, "That Jewish wife thing was just a phase." That's what her sister-in-law does, and really, you can't blame her. But Ruth doesn't do that. Instead, she decides that she is going to tie her circumstances to Naomi's. She chooses to live in a way that makes Naomi's problems her problems, that makes Naomi's prayers her prayers, that makes Naomi's lament her lament.

Ruth then goes on to center Naomi in her life. Naomi may be the poor old widow who needs help, but she is also the one who has the most intimate knowledge about how the society and the system they need to function in works. Ruth encourages Naomi to be the expert in her own story. We need to heed this example. It is very easy for the people with the most options to assume that they know the best ways not only to live their own lives but also to make decisions for people who have fewer choices because of where they live or their financial situation—or just their general spot in the hierarchy of society. But people are experts at their own lives. We need to be with others, we need to support them and help them, but we don't need to take over. Ruth decides to attach her life to Naomi's, saying, "Where you go I will go" (Ruth 1:16). Ruth does so because Naomi needs her, and she loves Naomi. Ruth loves her neighbor as herself and ties their outcomes together. We need to do this with people who have less privilege than we do. Just as Ruth is ultimately blessed by being a blessing to another, I believe we too will be blessed by lamenting with our neighbors—not for them, but *with* them, by tying our lives to their lives. When we are truly with one another and share banks and grocery stores and schools—and one another's burdens—we all are blessed.

Ruth is not the only one who knows how to be with others in her story. First Ruth decides to be with Naomi, and then a man named Boaz decides to be hospitable to strangers. Because Boaz is faithful to God, he provides for people who need care. Ruth and Naomi are gleaning in Boaz's field when he first lays eyes on Ruth. They are only able to be there because Boaz harvested as Leviticus instructs, leaving enough for those who need it. I can imagine that Boaz's generosity created a tiny community, that every year during harvest, the same people would come to the fields they knew would have extra. It would be easy for Boaz to spot Ruth because he knew the normal gleaners. He immediately recognizes that, as a woman, she would need more protection and tells his servants to protect her. He thinks of anyone gleaning his fields as his neighbor and sides with them. When we are with people, their struggles begin to matter to us. We cannot care about everything, and we certainly can't *do* everything about every problem we encounter. But we can deeply impact those around us by crying out on their behalf, by lamenting the ways that our neighbors are not cared for, and by encouraging our government to take care of the least of these.

Boaz helps Ruth and Naomi because there is margin in his life, in his field, in the ways that he operates. He follows the law of Leviticus, which tells him to leave enough for those who really need it, and therefore has room in his life to be with them. He is with them in the ways that he accepts his responsibility toward Ruth and Naomi as his neighbors. He rightly sees them as a gift instead of a burden. Ruth chooses to be with Naomi in her struggles, to advocate and lament with her. Naomi shows Ruth the ways of her community, and Boaz is blessed because he cares about the lament of these women. When we lament with people, we are blessed by God.

Practice Makes (Im)Perfect

The most helpful practical tool I have found for being with others is the circle of grief. This tool is a way to recognize who needs to care for whom in a tough circumstance. It looks like a circle with a circle drawn around it, and a circle drawn around that, and another circle drawn around that. You can have as many concentric circles as you want. The person with the problem is in the middle. Then the person who is most affected by that person's pain is in the next circle, and so on and so on. When my dad went into the hospital for seizures, he was in the center of the circle of grief, then my mom was right outside of that, then I was right outside of that because I was the daughter who drove in from out of town. My sisters were right outside of my circle, and everyone else was outside of my sisters' circle.

If the circle of grief flows correctly, care goes into the circle and lament goes out. I am not going to ask my mom to hold the pain of me not being with my kids, or that it is inconvenient to work from her house because she has enough going on. That lament of mine goes to my sisters, or my husband, or my friends. Meanwhile, it is not OK for my sisters to complain to me about how they wish they were here. I can't hold that right now, but there are people on the outside of their circle who can. Meanwhile, care goes in. I feed my mom, my mom gets my dad's stuff ready to go to the hospital, my sisters send me a Starbucks gift card, and my sisters' friends send them cards and put us all on the prayer list.

In a good, solid community, there are lots of circles and the help goes in and the pain/complaining goes out. The person who has cancer should not hear about how bummed you are that she is missing your wedding. But that also is a bummer, so complain to your bridesmaid about it. The feelings aren't bad. We should feel whatever we feel, but make sure you are aiming those feelings in an appropriate direction. They need to go to a safe place, a place that won't hurt other people. Communal lament is powerful, but if we are always centering ourselves, we are not loving our neighbor.

Sometimes when we lament with others, it can feel like there is no room for us to lament our own traumas. God is *always* big enough to hold all our feelings. When we trust God with our feelings, we can have more space to hold the feelings of other people. Sometimes when other people are having a hard time, it can be easy to say, "But I am having a hard time too!" It wasn't just that Naomi had lost her sons; Ruth had lost her husband. Everyone grieved, but Ruth centered Naomi, and that allowed their stories to unfold in a beautiful way across generations. We need to know who is the most vulnerable and always be thinking of their lament.

Take a look at your own life. Who in your neighborhood is the most vulnerable? Who are the kids in the school system you live in who are hungry and behind a reading level? What are you an expert at and what connections do you have? Is your life even set up so that you could lament with others? Do you have the time and emotional space to hear other people? What would it take to get those things in order?

Lamenting with others isn't easy. It is extremely inconvenient, and it is totally worth it. It is where God shows up over and over and where all of us can be made new together.

Prayer

Decentering yourself is deeply countercultural. Everything about America says, "What about *me?!*" Our individualism is well documented and almost always running rampant. My prayer for you is that you learn the power of centering the lives and stories of people who are not like you. May you learn the beauty of yoking your life to the lives of those on the margins.

Part Three

PUBLIC LAMENT AS AN AGENT OF CHANGE

7

WE WILL NOT BE SILENT

Lament Is Speaking Truth to Power

I f personal lament helps our relationship with God and lament in a community makes us better together, crying out in public against the injustices of this world gives us a shot at ushering in the kingdom of God Jesus is always talking about. Public lament is the cries of not just those who are being hurt by personal circumstances or within a community but those whose human worth is being disregarded at a systemic level. It is also the cries of those who are not being oppressed but who choose to join their neighbors who are being hurt by the systems that our lives are entrenched within. Just like we have to process our personal trauma in order to work through it, we must process our collective trauma in order to become a better world. Lament allows us to first recognize and then process the wrongness of this world so that we may work with God to make it right.

In biblical times, disrupting society to show the suffering of the marginalized and oppressed was a holy calling. The people howling and making a scene as a personal public protest were called prophets. They screamed and cried and lay naked in the streets. They called the people in power names. They reminded the Hebrew people about what God wanted from them and insisted that God's people do better, especially for the poor, the refugee, the racial minority, the widow.

Old Testament prophets were often sent to disrupt lives, to literally lie in the street, to make fires out of poop and stink up the place, to marry prostitutes. Seriously, they actually did those things. This is perhaps why Ezekiel and Hosea are generally left out of children's Sunday school curriculums. These stunts were a way for them to lament the way the world worked. Essentially, it was their way of saying, "What you are doing stinks! So here, I am going to make the town stink." The prophets are rarely subtle. They did extremely weird stuff so that other people would begin talking about the wrongs of this world.

The prophets spoke truth to power. The prophet Elisha made a military leader go wash in the Jordan seven times likes a commoner. Jesus braided a whip (I wonder how long that took) so he could cause a serious disturbance in the temple. All this was done to call out a wrong and to get the people to pay attention to the hurt of this world. And we love these stories! We love the idea of a disturbance, but we feel differently about the reality of it. Just imagine for a second that someone interrupted your church service to chase the ushers around as they collected the offering. I don't think the finance chairs would be keen on that.

A few years ago, I attended a church service on the east side of Atlanta at a church I love dearly. One of their stated values was to be justice-oriented and inclusive. In this service, after the sermon but before Communion, there was an unexpected interruption. Right as we were passing the peace, someone walked in from the back of our church and began proclaiming that the rugs in the building were stolen from his home. He hollered about how this church had hurt him and he wanted justice. He was mistaken—the church bought those rugs off Amazon like most of us do—but no one that was there will ever forget it. I have been to church almost every Sunday of my entire life, and that was the first time I heard someone interrupt.

The church handled this interruption well, mostly because they had a staff member trained in de-escalation, but to me, it was a stark reminder that church is literally the last place we expect anything out of the ordinary to happen. When it does, disturbances end quickly so we can return to the status quo. Lament is almost always inconvenient. It takes an extreme amount of effort to build a church service that encourages public lament. When it happens, we need to learn to make room for it, to welcome the interruption and think of it as a cue from the Holy Spirit to pay attention. Usually, there is no space to hear about the ways the church has ignored the hurts of this world. But shouldn't there be room in the church for public lament? I long for a church that seeks to hear about wrongs and correct those injustices.

Do We Hear the People Cry?

Those who ask for something from people in power are almost always accused of being angry. If someone is angry, then the powers that be don't have to do what those angry people want. Weeping and gnashing of teeth equal hysteria, and it's all too easy to undermine people who are "hysterical." These accusations are used to police and silence lament. Mostly, the people accused of being "angry" aren't white. Mostly, the people accused of being "hysterical" are women. By labeling other people's lament with these negative labels, we dismiss it, refusing to hear the hurt, let alone do something about it. Often people who are being told they need to be civil are simply lamenting. And the Bible makes a pretty clear case for their right to be mad. Psalm 137 is an incredibly angry psalm from a people who are oppressed. It is a response to the oppressor who demands that they just pipe down and be happy. Speaking up is what they do instead; it is presented as a holy response.

I've been called angry many times, but my first distinct memory of it happened on the bus in the third grade. I didn't like the boy in front of me calling girls stupid and weak. I said something. The boy told me I was already an angry feminist. It was said as though that was a bad thing. I remember knowing that feminist was an insult and that I should be ashamed. I grew up knowing that my temper was a problem, that my bursts of anger needed to be controlled, and that it was not OK for little girls to demand things.

Later, as I grew into my femininity, I learned to wield my anger in ways that were more socially acceptable. I grew "concerned." I learned how to express my anger at the unjust world in a way that would be heard, and I learned to demand meetings with the manager. Because I am white and presently able-bodied and middle class, I was not ignored. Well, I was once, but then my husband stepped in, signing his name "Dr. Norman." We got what we wanted, but I feel like you already knew that part. It didn't bother anyone how mad my husband got. He had a PhD and a severe lack of melanin, so he was allowed to get angry. His anger is always justified to society. My anger is considered less justified, but my Black female friend (who is correct far more often than I am) is almost always told she is too angry to be heard.

"If you asked nicely, we would stop hurting you": this is a lie that our society tells in about a thousand different ways. People with power use the word *civility*. We ask people to talk nicely, or we refuse to engage. We say, "Hey! I understand that you 'feel passionately' about that, but don't you know that they won't hear you if you yell?"—as though yelling was the first thing they did. Here's the thing: before anyone publicly laments, they have usually already tried everything else. People yell "Black Lives Matter!" because our society has not heard all the calls that have come before. If you see someone yelling in the streets, assume they already asked nicely. Then think about whether violence in low-income neighborhoods and a collection of laws that guarantee that schools will not properly educate the kids in them are really just things that you have to ask about nicely in order to see real change happen. The protests and demands to be treated as full members of our society come from a place of deep pain, from generations of always being told to wait quietly and ask nicely while suffering and systemic injustice run amok.

Everybody gets to lament, and everybody gets to lament loudly and publicly. That's how it should be, but it's not how society tends to work. When white people attempt to police the lament of minorities, especially Black people, they love to quote Rev. Dr. Martin Luther King Jr. They like "I Have a Dream." White people don't hear the later stuff that would make them uncomfortable. After the famous speech, King lamented the attitudes of white moderates. He said that white people asking people to be civil and wait patiently for equality were doing more harm than those marching with the Ku Klux Klan. When he said that little Black boys and little Black girls mattered as much as white ones nicely, the white people nodded along, even said yes in public, but were unwilling to make any changes that cost them anything. When Martin Luther King Jr. got louder, he was killed.

People in power who refuse to listen to hurting people until they publicly protest do not have the right to tell the demonstrators that their demonstrations are inappropriate. People in power do not have the right to tell someone who is hurting how they should cry out. We don't have the right to say what would make that person feel better, because we don't know. We don't have the right to say how and when we want to hear the message that we need to change, to demand that people work around our comfort. Disruptive protest practices aren't a typical first move. By the time disruption happens, you can be pretty sure the protesters already tried asking, but you wouldn't hear them because you were too comfortable. Change is hard, and most humans don't change unless they have to. Comfort and power are very, very easy to get used to. Sometimes yelling is necessary to be heard. Even if it is not, people who are hurting have a right to tell their own story in their own way. Very often, the message isn't civil because the reality of our world isn't civil either. Lament demands that we see the injustice so that we might work with God to make the world just.

Raging against What's Normal

How do we bear witness in a world that tries to hide the suffering of the most oppressed? How do we honor the public laments of the suffering and join our voices to them? The most obvious answer is, we listen. We pay attention to which voices we are hearing and which ones we are not, and we listen to the voices that make us uncomfortable. When we do this, we can recognize the unjust systems we participate in and join the hard work of dismantling those systems with our laments.

One of my dearest friends left an abusive relationship right about when we first began hanging out together at the pool for the summer. We would watch our kids splash around, reapply sunscreen, and share snacks as the kids wore themselves out and the sun beat down. In the way that people who have one eye on their kids do, we got to know one another. We talked about our lives and our marriages. We talked about our kids' activities and what we were watching on Netflix. We talked about how hard life was when you are the caregiver for children and also have your own big dreams. Sometimes we would shrug and say, "It is just hard." Parenting is hard, being a grown-up is hard, marriage is hard. Then one of our kids would demand that we watch for the seventy-eighth time as they cannon-balled off the side of the pool.

What I didn't know when we were sitting in the pool was that our definitions of hard were very, very different. My hard was the basic issues of living with another adult and having to consider them and their feelings. Her hard was "I am afraid for my safety and the safety of my child on a regular basis, and I preemptively do everything I can to make sure my husband never gets mad." I had absolutely no idea.

As the stories slowly trickled out in the months and years that followed, my heart broke for her every time. Why didn't she tell me sooner? Why did I not know how bad it was? At first, she shrugged and said she wasn't sure. Later, when she had processed some of her pain in therapy and had some distance from the abuse, she could explain it. "Abby," she said, "you know how everyone says that marriage is hard?" Yeah, I nodded. "I guess I thought that this was just my hard. I just thought this was marriage-hard." She thought being afraid every day was what it meant for a marriage to be hard. I was talking about how neither of us wanted to get up to get the baby for the third time that night and that we had to feed the family every day and that there was a never-ending mountain of laundry. She was talking about living in gut-wrenching fear and pain. We hadn't defined it because we didn't think we needed to. Both of us thought our situations were "normal" because they were our normal. They were what we were used to.

Humans have an amazing capacity to normalize things. It is an evolutionary response that keeps us alive. We think of continuous circumstances in our lives as normal so that we can constantly assess new threats. But this also means that we stop thinking of dangerous or unjust systems as a threat. Instead, they become normal.

Lament is the tool that we possess to call out the ways of this world that hurt us and hurt our neighbors. It is the first step in correcting the wrongs that our society quietly deems OK. Lament shows us that when we have become complacent toward injustice, we need to repent. Lament in the public square reminds the world that it was never God's plan for less than everyone to thrive. We need to be specific in our language of injustice. We need to be able to name the ugly things so that people know they are not OK. We need to let people who have been a part of a sinful world their entire existence know that it doesn't have to hurt in all these ways. This is why we lament and why we do it in public.

We also run the risk of normalizing systemic oppression in our society. When we live within systemic oppression, we think it is normal. It is amazing what we can get used to as a society. It is really astounding what becomes normal. I have sat and talked with people, still alive, who lived most of their lives with separate water fountains based on race. When you ask them about it, they tell you it was normal. I always thought that was so strange. Surely my mom thought it was weird that she didn't know a person of color until college. "Nope," she would say with a shrug. "Pretty typical for small-town Indiana." *No way*, I would think, *I will never be like that.*

I was in high school when the Columbine shooting happened. It rocked America. It rocked me. We would talk about it in class, figure out an escape route, wonder if it could ever happen in our school. It seemed so strange. Someone bringing a gun into a school felt impossible. Surely this would never happen again. The national conversation was very much about prevention: How could this happen? How can we make sure this never happens again? This cannot happen again—that was the cry. They locked every door, and we could no longer sneak out through the band hallway for lunch. Trench coats and book bags must stay in lockers in case we were hiding weapons. Still, school shootings continued.

By the time I got my own classroom, five years after I graduated high school, intruder drills and how to minimize death if we experienced a shooting were part of the new faculty orientation. I now have elementary schoolchildren who find intruder drills totally normal. I have a ten-year-old who has spent her entire elementary school career being occasionally interrupted so that she and her classmates can practice hiding under desks and in bathrooms. She sees it the same way I saw fire drills: just a thing that interrupts the day. But when I have an active shooter plan for my congregation and my kids come home talking about "bad-guy drills," something is wrong. This should not be normal.

Before we can have the world God desires for us, we first need to name the things that are not OK. We must lament a reality where our kids are not safe. We must lament the fact that our country cares more about Second Amendment rights than second grade teachers' lives. We must lament that Black people are still being shot in the streets, the ways that things have still not changed despite the cries of civil rights leaders. We must cry out to God and to the powers that be so that things will change.

When looking at systemic problems, it can feel totally overwhelming to know what to do first. No one wants the world to be unjust, but it is. No one wants public shootings to be a reality, but they are. We can feel powerless against these nameless, faceless systems. Lament reminds us that things should be changed and can be.

One of the things that makes my husband grow extremely angry and run off on a tirade is when people shrug at injustice and say, "It's the policy," as if the policy is a thing that is separate from the people who create it. But if we say, "It's just the policy," then no one has any control, no one has any responsibility, and no one can change anything. It just . . . is. But that isn't good enough. Public lament is the time we say, "*No!* No, it is unacceptable to lock kids in cages. No, we do not charge fourteen-year-olds as adults. No, we do not let low-income kids have subpar educations." Systems need to change, but first, we have to say, and say loudly, "This is not right!" Lament lays claim to what is not right in the world, and it holds people responsible for the way our society is set up. Lament says that we should do better, we can do better, that you are capable of better.

The prophetic work of the church and the individuals within it is to remind the world that this is not normal. It is not normal to hurt like this. You can in fact heal. There is a better way. You do not have to be in pain. But in order to show people that there is a better way, we have to acknowledge that what we have right now isn't enough. It is a sign of a broken world that our kids have to practice running from a gunman in their school. Other countries don't do that, and we could be different. In order to get people to believe things could be different, we have to publicly say that the way things are now is bad. It grieves God, and it grieves us as God's people. We show this to the world by lamenting in places where others can see us and hear us. We need to lament because we believe that people *can* change, that systems *can* change because God can change us if we repent. This is what lament does for us. Lament changes the world because lament changes us, but we have to participate in it. We have to let it change us.

It *Is* Your Problem

One of the rallying cries of liberal women and especially modern moms is "There is no such thing as other people's children" (I think Glennon Melton started it). I love the idea because it recognizes the image of God in each of us. "There is no such thing as other peoples' children" is a beautiful lament. But it only works as a lament if we are willing to also call ourselves out and root out our own complicity in systems that let some children have everything they need and others go without.

"There is no such thing as other peoples' children" is much easier to say when people call out the injustices against children who are far from them because those are injustices that they are not complicit in. It is a different thing when the injustice is very close to you. When there are children a million miles away who cannot eat, well, that is a tragedy. But what about the kids in the literal next school district over who are also hungry *and* whose parents cannot share the burden for rotating snack duty because they don't have the extra money in the food budget? That is also a tragedy, one that could be fixed by the redistricting people fight against because it hurts their property value.

Lamenting injustice should be about not just those things out there but the things here we benefit from, the things we could change with our time, our money, our votes, our influence. Usually when the school district lines are redrawn, the richer people claim that they should *not* be; they claim that there are good reasons to leave them the way they are. I am talking about not just my neighborhood or my city (although I suppose I could) but rather in every city in America. This injustice is happening everywhere; it is probably happening in your neighborhood. If you lament that injustice, you are inviting God to change you so that you take steps to repent.

We need lament to make sure we remember what God wants. We are born as sinners into a fallen world; even the language that we inherit is infected with sin. Even the way we construct our thoughts about the world is not perfect. Lament removes the lenses that we have been given by the world and allows us to replace them with God's eyes. We lament so that we can step back and look at the ways our society is set up and how we are positioned in it. For lots of us, that means acknowledging our privilege. Privilege is something that we inherit based on our position in the world. It may not be our fault, exactly, that being white or male or straight or cisgender gives us a leg up on our fellow human beings, but it is definitely our problem.

Lament, especially public lament, allows us to say that our position is wrong, that other people being treated as less-than is not OK in the eyes of our God. Lament holds us accountable for the actions we take to divest in our own privilege. It is hard, yes, but it is the way we work toward a better world. We need to name what is broken so that people know it is not supposed to be that way.

Collectively Advocating for the Marginalized

The church was once a place where people who were on the outskirts of society could come to and be treated with the dignity of bearing God's image no matter what. It did not matter if you were a widow, or a beggar, or born with some sort of disfigurement. It was a place where women could be heard and the enslaved were freed.

In the beginning, the church was a radical place. People with disabilities and women who had no other value in society flocked to the church because the church was so different from the rest of the world. The widow and the wounded were valued in the early church because God values everyone, especially those who were in the margins. Unfortunately, the church has lost its prophetic place in the world. The church now much more often reflects the harsh realities of the economics of the day, not the heart of God. We sometimes like to pretend that is some sort of glitch in the system, that the American church just needs some minor awakening to be the beacon of light to the world Jesus described in the Sermon on the Mount.

I wish this were the case. I was reminded recently—through my relationship with Shannon Dingle, a disability activist within the church—that when the Americans with Disabilities Act (ADA) was passed, the church in America spent an ungodly amount of money to make sure that it was exempt from the laws. Churches made sure they didn't have to have wheelchair ramps or bathrooms that accommodated all God's people. There are very few churches that are accommodating or accessible. This is a travesty. This was a time when the church could have stood up and didn't. I believe this grieves God. We need to lament worrying about money and keeping people out. We need to publicly state that we were wrong, that we have not lived up to the call that Jesus put to the church.

Sometimes it feels like change is impossible. Who are we that we can change anything? We are just individuals with limited resources and influence. Lament, especially group lament, is about telling the truth to the people who can do something about the injustices of our world. Lament is very much about speaking truth to power. We do not have the capabilities to fix the health crisis, the price of insulin, the inequalities in education. It is in fact out of our control to fix systemic racism. But we can say to the people who can change it that it needs to be changed. We can get our friends to join us in the outcry. We can holler at the person (or the God) that has the power to turn on the faucet and fill our cup.

One of the most powerful voices of lament in America is Rev. Dr. William Barber. He has restarted a movement that was a centerpiece of Rev. Dr. Martin Luther King Jr.'s work. Dr. Barber's The Poor People's Campaign is always asking, "How will these laws, these policies, these new programs affect the poorest among us?" Rev. Dr. Barber leads protests and lobbies Congress because America is currently unjust, and he wants everyone to be advocated for. This is the work of lament: saying what is wrong in our world. Yes, the bill someone has introduced is covering people who are too sick to work, but it does not cover people who are part of the gig economy. It does not cover the people who are unable to work to begin with. The lament that the Poor People's Campaign partakes in points to those who are otherwise ignored and says, "Forgetting anyone is wrong, and that is what is currently happening."

It was from Rev. Dr. Barber that I learned that a budget is a moral document. It tells us what and who matter the most. What does your city budget look like? Who is most represented? What does your church budget look like? Is it available? What about your local school budget? How much is allocated to making sure the kids with no resources get what they need? A politician will tell you what he hopes will happen; a budget will tell you who gets prioritized when hard decisions need be made. It is our job to lament publicly so that no one will be forgotten, so that none of the children in our cities are considered "other people's children." Lament is the first step in that work; it points out the problem.

Lament as an Agent of Change

The prophet Ezekiel spends a lot of time telling the Israelites what they are doing wrong in truly bizarre ways. He eats a scroll as part of a public art performance. He lies naked in the street on one of his sides, then flips to his other side and lies there for another forty days. He is doing all this ridiculous stuff to point out that the temple is not being put in its rightful place and that God is not being honored. Ezekiel is very specific when he talks about what is wrong so that he can explain how good it could be. He makes a list and he sticks to it. He makes sure people understand. I want a church that is a dog with a bone when it comes to fixing injustices. It's time to start being serious about not just naming the things that are happening but imagining what it will look like when those things no longer exist.

A group of women in Oakland, California, decided they needed to lament publicly. They were displaced by the extreme spikes in rent. They had nowhere to live. They were losing their community while the apartments sat empty. They decided that they needed to be heard. When they were evicted, they stayed. They squatted. They forced the powers that be to hear them. They did not leave quietly. They stayed and cried out and gave facts and figures and demanded to be heard. And then finally, they were heard. The people of the city figured out a way for them to stay, for their children not to have their lives displaced, and for the people who were truly in need to get what they required. That thing your mom used to say about how where there is a will, there is a way—sometimes it's true. When we lament together, we are heard. When we cry out together, we can let God work through all of us to make a change.

My ten-year-old came home a few months ago speaking about Emmet Till, whom she learned about at school. She learned that he was beaten to death and that his mama decided to have an open-casket funeral. She learned that he didn't do anything wrong, but that if he did, it was simply whistling at a white girl (later in her life, this woman admitted that even that minor "slight" had been fabricated). I discovered she learned all this because I listened as she told her little sister all about it. I sat frozen in the front seat of the car as my girls discussed this horrible piece of American history. I wasn't sure they were ready. I didn't want them to have to think about it. I didn't want them, as white girls, to hear stories where white girls were the villains. I was deeply uncomfortable, and I just wanted everyone to stop talking and continue singing whatever musical soundtrack we had playing on the car radio. But I also knew that all those feelings were diametrically opposed to the world I want my girls to grow up in and to the kinds of women I want them to be. More than I want them to not be sad or bothered, I want them to grow up to work toward living in a just world and lament with those who lament.

Emmet Till's story is known still today because his mother, Mamie Till-Mobley, insisted that the world confront the reality of her son's body. She demanded an open-casket funeral and invited the press. Mrs. Till-Mobley decided that telling the truth about the reality of Black people in America was more important than anyone's comfort. Remembering this mother, I kept quiet. I asked the girls, as white girls, what they thought about the girl in the story. I (gently) told them stuff like this still happens, and even though it isn't fair, any accusation they make against Black people will probably be taken a lot more seriously than those made by the Black girls in their class. Bearing witness to the pain of Mamie Till-Mobley, to the reality of Emmet Till, made me want to crawl under the front seat of the van, but the girls took it in stride.

Their readiness to listen and learn reminded me, once again, that we tend to use our children's comfort as an excuse for civility—that they are in fact ready to hear the truth of the world. We tell ourselves we cannot expose our children to bad things when what we really want is to not have to face them ourselves, to not have to answer those blunt children's questions, to not have to sit with the discomfort of a lamenting world. Children understand what lament is for. They want to know what is wrong so they can fix it. We don't need to be untruthful or to hide our kids from pain. Instead, we need to teach them to hear and heed the lament of this world.

Pretending that things are OK when they absolutely are not is actually a sin in the eyes of our God. Refusing to hear lament and refusing to change the systems of the world so that they don't kill innocent children because they are Black grieves God. Mamie Till-Mobley was standing on a deep biblical precedent by weeping in a way that her pain could be heard. A mother crying out publicly for her son dying too young at the hands of the state is something we must bear witness to until it doesn't happen anymore.

Lamenting Systemic Oppression Is Holy: The Bible Tells Me So

One of the most powerful scenes of lament in the Bible is the scene of the crucifixion depicted in the Gospel of John. I love all of John 17–19, but I especially love the bits about Mary, the mother of Jesus, lamenting at the cross. John writes, "Meanwhile, standing near the cross of Jesus were his mother, and his mother's sister, Mary the wife of Clopas, and Mary Magdalene. When Jesus saw his mother and the disciple whom he loved standing beside her, he said to his mother, 'Woman, here is your son.' Then he said to the disciple, 'Here is your mother.' And from that hour the disciple took her into his own home" (John 19:25–27 NRSV). I can't help but see Mary in the same vein as Mamie Till-Mobley and, more contemporarily, the Mothers of the Movement. Women, mothers of children who were shot or killed by police officers or by gun violence. Mothers who watched as their children were turned into hashtags and as the death of their son or daughter came to represent so much more than just one tragedy. Women who saw their child die and then watched as their grief was put on display and as the state labeled their children "a thug," "a criminal," "disrespectful," "noncompliant," all in an effort to explain away the horrors done to them. I cannot help but see Mary, mother of Jesus as first in line among them: Sybrina Fulton, Lezley McSpadden, Gwen Carr, Geneva Reed-Veal, Cleopatra Pendleton-Cowley, Maria Hamilton, Lucy McBath.

Mary, mother of Jesus, watched her son die. The account of the crucifixion in John could not be clearer. She was there, and Jesus knew that, commented on it even. While the soldiers cast lots for his clothes, and the chief priests and Pilate were already fighting over the narrative that would be told about his death, Mary stood by and watched her child die. Her baby, the one she felt leap in her womb, the one whose birth she would never, ever forget, the child who nearly gave her a heart attack when he did not follow directions and stick close by when she lost him in the temple. The child who had been talked about since before his birth and certainly since the strange circumstances at the manger.

Yes, God's only son was sent to earth to save humanity by dying on a cross at Calgary. But Mary still watched her firstborn child slowly fade away as he was tortured by the state, mostly to make a point about what was and was not acceptable Jewish behavior. She watched while they talked about what to do with his cloak, as though he was already gone. And Mary stood in public and wept, wept at the sight of her firstborn son being crucified. She stood at the cross and wept. She wanted people to see her lament. It was public. She wanted people to know what had happened to her son at the hands of the state. Her lament is noticed even by Jesus while he is dying. It is recorded in the Bible, and it expanded the story. When we cannot understand anything else, we can understand the lament of a mother.

Practice Makes (Im)Perfect

I know it is very, very easy to say, "Look, I can't call out every injustice, so I should just quit before I begin. If I call one injustice out, don't I have to call all them out? That seems exhausting!" But as you learn to be honest with God about how you are feeling, and also hang out with people and learn to lament as though your neighbors' problems are your own, I believe your heart will change. Imagine what a church would look like if it were full of people who knew what they felt and also what grieved their neighbor. What a radical church that would be indeed! I want to go to a church like that; I want to hang out with people like that!

In order to start the process of lamenting systemic injustices, we must start somewhere. What is the thing that breaks your heart? Food insecurity, medical inequality, foster kids being treated poorly—find something that makes you stay awake at night and learn all about it. Then lament all about it. For me, that thing is inequality in education. I hate it. I hate it so much. So I joined my local Parent Teacher Association even before my kids were in school. I raise money for the classrooms, and I have a relationship with the teachers. I have the school social worker on speed dial, and when she calls, I answer. Then I take what I have and bother the people within my reach to get the socks, the underwear, the water, the winter coats, whatever it is she says she needs. Together, we make a massive difference. Answering my phone and bothering people on Twitter are the things I am good at. I invite others into the lament in my heart.

Maybe your thing that makes your heart break is that not everyone can have a green space. Maybe your thing is that not everyone has access to fresh vegetables. Maybe you don't know what your thing is. Ask God to break your heart about something. Research it. Figure it out. Talk to people about it. Put your literal money where your mouth is. Let God show you the plight of the people in your own city. Let that change you. Allow yourself to lament.

Prayer

May we see clearly the ways that we are complicit in the system. May you be brave enough to ask God to convict you. May you change. May you call out the systems that are hurting your neighbors and be brave enough to imagine a more holy world.

CONCLUSION

Lament as Revealing the Heart of God

We Lament So We Can Imagine a New World Together

God constantly invites us to a new way, and always, the first step of that invitation is to lament the way things are now. We live in a world where the kingdom of God is coming and also the kingdom of God is here. We need to act like it is possible that all people could live together well. Howard Thurman called this "the beloved community," and it sits at the heart of the civil rights movement. A movement that fought for a world in which all people have the same rights and chances, that led public lament because everyone wasn't being treated as a beloved child of God. I believe our imagination is our greatest asset when it comes to seeing how the ways of the world can change into the ways of God, but we cannot get there if we first do not understand that God isn't happy about the way things are now. We lament so that we can then imagine a better way.

The prophet Micah's name means "who is like Yahweh." People who claim to be children of God need to answer that question. Are we? Are we being like the God we confess or are we instead relying on the way the world works and shrugging our shoulders? I love the metaphor most Protestant churches have of a totally open table. The Communion table is God's table, and everyone is invited. We practice serving one tiny meal the way that God would want us to serve it.

When my family switched churches, we moved from one that gave Communion only to the believers to one that welcomed even little children to the table. I had a lot of feelings about this. While I understood it in theory, I wasn't sure if it was OK that my kid was taking Communion. I had no idea what the first sermon was about because I spent the entire time freaking out about the Communion I knew was coming. Right before I stood up, I sent up a frantic prayer to God: "OK, God, is it OK for someone to take Communion when they really don't understand your grace and the resurrection and what it all stands for?" I swear I could immediately hear God laughing. "Oh," God said to me, "you think you understand everything that happens at the Communion table? You think you have wrapped your mind around grace and forgiveness and everything that happened at the cross?" I took my daughter to go receive Communion. I needed to lament and repent of the hardness in my own heart so that I could participate with my daughter in this beautiful meal.

My other daughter also had a dramatic First Communion. She told me she didn't want to take it, so I left her in the pew. She sometimes takes longer to make up her mind. She finally decided she *did* want to take Communion right when they were putting up the elements. She began crying, afraid that she was too late, that she had missed it. She was afraid there was a time limit on the table being open. I grabbed her weeping body and took her up to the table, where a woman and man smiled at her even though they were inconvenienced. They walked back to the table, took the elements carefully back down, and scrunched down to her. "This," our pastor said, "is a reminder that Jesus loves you so, so much." Then the cup was moved to her level as a smiling face said to her, "And this is a reminder that Jesus is always with you." I don't think she remembers that, but I hope I never forget it. I hope the kingdom of God is always represented as open even when inconvenient, available to crying girls who took too long to decide whether they wanted to participate. I hope we offer God's grace to one another always at the wrong time with smiling faces as a reminder that Jesus is here with us. I hope that our lament is met with an invitation to the Lord's supper and a reminder that Jesus loves us even when we are inconvenient.

Micah, the book of the Bible describing the prophet's life, has a happy ending. His lament and call to repentance work. People hear him. People change. People do things a better way, and then the judgment of the Lord is delayed for a century. But this didn't happen right away. A section in the third part of Micah is a court scene. In this scene, Micah pleads with God to hang on, to wait a minute before passing final judgment, to give the people more time. Micah gets that time because God holds hope that people will change. God does not want to judge our communities, and that's good news. God instead longs for us to be invited into a better way.

In the Methodist liturgy of Communion, we start by confessing that we have not loved one another or God as we should. Then the liturgist gets to announce the good news, that Jesus came for us, that God has not forgotten us, that in the name of Jesus, *you are forgiven!* God wants us to live fuller lives. God wants the world to be a better place. God designed us, and our relationship with one another, and our churches to be the bearers of that incredible news. The good news is that God wants to be in a full relationship with us, that we can trust God when we need to lament to God. The good news is that we can be with one another and have a fuller picture of community if we are willing to lament with one another. The good news is that God longs for the world to change, and it can. But that only happens if we are willing to call out the wrongs that we see now in order to point to a better way.

One of the most striking scenes in the Bible is when Mary Magdalene comes to the tomb, oils in hand, to bury Jesus. She is not hoping for anything. She is deep in grief. When she gets there, she finds that the body is gone. The small comfort of preparing the body has also been taken from her. She is lamenting in the garden when Jesus appears to her. She is ready to bury her Savior but instead discovers there is new life on the other side.

I believe that each of us, at least once in our lives, is like Mary Magdalene. We are deep in mourning. The world is not how we thought it was. We are angry and sad and even the smallest comfort has been taken from us. We do not know how we can go on. Like Mary Magdalene, we must face our own grief. We must go and be prepared to bury our greatest hopes. But I also believe that Jesus meets us in that place of lament. I believe Jesus calls to each of us, "Why are you weeping?" and I believe that if we can just find the answer to that question, Jesus will show us the way to new life. Lament is how we get to Jesus and the glories of a world as God always intended.

BENEDICTION

Dear Reader,

Lament is not an easy subject to grapple with. Lamenting to God, lamenting with others, and lamenting the brokenness of our world is hard, deep work. I am proud of you for being willing to go there. I am sure God is moving in you so that you might move in this world. May God continue to be with you as you engage with yourself and with the world.

So dear and brave friends who have decided to learn about the holy work of lament, if you would allow me, it would be my greatest blessing to pray for you. As a pastor, I must confess, the benediction is my favorite part of every service I have ever preached. So imagine me in my collar and my bright-red lipstick, my eyes shut tight behind my cat-eye glasses and one hand held in the air, hovering over your head, as I cry,

May you go into the world trusting the God who sees you just as Hag-gai trusted the God who saw her. May you feel known and validated in your deepest struggles and greatest heartaches. May you always know that you are not alone, that God is with you, that God sees you.

May you go into the world with the willingness of Ruth, to lament with others, to see their pain, to identify with them. May your heart break for those who are not like you, for those who have been forgotten by the powers and principalities of this world. May your presence remind them that Jesus is Emmanuel—God with us. May you cry hot tears over other people's suffering. May you be filled with a compassion that will draw you closer to God.

May you go into the world crying out, weeping like the Holy Mother herself, broken at the sight of her child being broken by the empire. May you weep and gnash your teeth and make a holy scene. May you refuse to get up out of the streets until the ways of the world are changed, until the most vulnerable among us are included, until the church means it when they say, "All are welcome, all are beloved by God."

May you go into this world lamenting like Mary Magdalene in the garden, who had been just hoping to bury her beloved rabbi. May Jesus meet you in the places of your deepest grief and invite you into a new and holy way of being, for the kingdom of God is coming, and the kingdom of God is here.

Amen.